hot nights cool days

First published in 2003 by New Holland Publishers (NZ) Ltd
Auckland • Sydney • London • Cape Town

218 Lake Road, Northcote, Auckland, New Zealand
14 Aquatic Drive, Frenchs Forest, NSW 2086, Australia
86-88 Edgware Road, London W2 2EA, United Kingdom
80 McKenzie Street, Cape Town 8001, South Africa

www.newhollandpublishers.co.nz

Copyright © 2003 in recipes: Julie Biuso
Copyright © 2003 in photography: Ian Batchelor
Copyright © 2003 New Holland Publishers (NZ) Ltd

ISBN: 1 86966 027 7

Publishing manager: Renée Lang
Design: Christine Hansen
Editor: Barbara Nielsen

Author photograph: courtesy of *Healthy Options* magazine

A catalogue record for this book is available from the National Library of
New Zealand

10 9 8 7 6 5 4 3 2 1

Colour reproduction by Colourscan (Singapore)
Printed in Hong Kong through Phoenix Offset, Hong Kong

hot nights cool days

Julie Biuso

Photography by **Ian Batchelor**

NEW HOLLAND

Dedication

Especially for my father, whose incredible good health has been an inspiration to me. The secret, he reckons, is in what he eats. He has always grown his own fruit and vegetables, and continues to do so. At 92 years old, he takes no pills for any ailments; food is still his only medicine.

Contents

Introduction

THE great thing about writing a cookbook is that you get to choose what you put in it. It means you get to *live* a little, to shop and cook and eat, to dabble in things that you might ordinarily have no business with, and to share all of this with your friends and family while ostensibly researching a book. There are worse jobs.

Hot Nights Cool Days has evolved over many summers spent at the beach, feeling the sand between my toes and the salt spray on my face, setting the pace for casual finger-licking food that is too scrumptious to ignore. Then there were the seemingly never-ending lunches enjoyed outside in dappled sunlight, and the early evening soirées under cerise sunsets streaked with gold. But this is not just a summer book. Once the leaves start to fall from the trees and indoors is the better place to be, *Hot Nights Cool Days* reveals its other side. Supping soup around the hearth, feeling the power of chilli as it ignites your mouth and makes your ears tingle, baking old favourites just the way Mum used to make them, and eating bowls of warming food that make you feel good inside – all these experiences come together in this book, too.

I still believe that home-cooked food is the best because you know what you're starting with, quite possibly where the food has come from, and what you're going to do to it. You have a relationship with it, too, as you think about what to buy, then choose it, handle it as you're preparing it and smell it as it cooks. And while food can be a great pleasure to enjoy and share, it can also be the key to feeling good and keeping well. Finding the balance takes some effort initially, but it can be achieved without too much of a compromise.

I've no time for the food police who want to take all the fun out of eating by banning anything with fat, salt, a speck of a carcinogen, or a shake of sugar. No one can convince me to throw away a piece of golden chicken skin, all crispy and crackling and begging to be eaten. It's a treat, and life without treats is boring. To counter the treats, you need to have a stash of goodies on the weekly menu. Fruit and vegetables are still top of the list, but it's about balance, not going without!

As for the recipes I've chosen, some are so delicious that my family has eaten them three nights on the trot to get our fill. Others are good working-horse recipes – the type that you can pull out of the bag midweek for a no-fuss meal. Some are just right show-offs, attention-grabbers that you can't ignore. And as for all those extra little bits of information – the comments and opinions, ideas for dishes to accompany, the best drink to serve alongside, and other tips you pick up but never write down (like kitchen utensils rattling around in a drawer, you can never find what you want when you need it), I've done my best to record everything I know, and to find out everything I didn't know, to bring the food alive in *your* kitchen.

It's a good feeling when you and your family or friends tuck into a meal you've cooked yourself, knowing that you're providing them with all the elements for good health along with that essential X-factor: pleasure.

JULIE BIUSO
www.juliebiuso.com

Kitchen lore

Titbits

Covers any anecdotal chitchat or historical references, and expands on practical procedures used in the method and things to watch out for. It may also include the sheer delight of a dish, sing its praises, and tell the reason why you just *have* to make it.

Pick up

Describes what you need to buy, what to look for in produce, and explains unusual ingredients.

Essential

Is the place for the mystery ingredient which will unlock the beauty of the dish – it's the key that brings it all together. It's often the one ingredient you should purchase ahead of others, and if you can't get it or afford it, perhaps you should look at making something else.

Alongside

Suggests ideas for other dishes which will make great plate mates before, after or alongside. It also recommends beverages to complement the food. Perhaps more importantly, there are hints about the mood, the setting, the fun aspect of the dish.

Up front

Tells what can be done in advance, something every cook wants to know. I've tried to be helpful here, not just in saying that a stew can be made a day ahead (because we all know that anyway), but that you can peel the garlic cloves, but not chop them (they would oxidise), and peel the oranges, but not slice them (they'd lose their juice), and roll the pastry, but not cook it (it's crisper the day it is baked), and weigh the cake ingredients and prepare the tin, and so on, the day before if you need to…helpful for those times when you're organising a big production and you know you'll be running around pulling your hair out on the day, and any little job you can do in advance is a godsend.

X-Factor

Gives the reason why you should eat this dish, whether it's because it is so good for you, and thankfully tastes fantastic, or for the hedonistic pleasure that eating naughty food occasionally gives us. In life, I think you need to strike a balance between the two. It's boring when you harp on about health all the time, but my overwhelming desire is to make people eat well by being aware of what they eat.

Hot stuff

Ovens are not created equal. Over time, you can develop an understanding for your oven's little idiosyncrasies – yes, it will have some. By choice, I prefer a hot oven. By that I mean an oven that will quickly reach the set temperature and maintain it without fluctuations. I like the thermostat to be accurate. If your oven doesn't cook food as quickly as you think it should, it could be that the thermostat needs adjusting. I like gas hobs because of the speed and control, but I prefer electric ovens. They seem to cook pastry better and brown meat more evenly. A fault of some gas ovens is the fluctuation in heat as the gas level rises and drops in an effort to maintain an even temperature. Having said that, I once had a cracker of a gas oven. It was old and built to last and roared along like a furnace. It was fabulous for meats, pies and pastry, bread and browning, but a disaster for cakes, meringues, crème brûlée and delicate foods. And that's the difficulty I have experienced with gas ovens, they're either too hot or they've got no real guts.

I like the fan-assisted option on my electric oven, but it doesn't suit all food. It gives an initial blast of high heat so the temperature comes up to speed very quickly, and it gives a nice dry heat. Excellent for pastry, superb for small joints of meat I want to cook quickly, but again, too hot and dry for cakes, meringues and delicate things.

Most cooks don't seem to address the difference between using the regular setting on an oven, and using the fan. Cooking on fanbake will increase the heat by around 10–15°C. A cake which should be cooked at 175°C on regular baking will develop a cracked top, burn or dry out if cooked on fanbake at 175°C (equivalent to 190°C). A chicken is much better cooked on a lower setting than on a 'fast cook' temperature because the high heat dries the surface flesh of the chicken and it loses its succulence. To avoid confusion, I've included the cooking option in brackets.

Measurements

Measuring is always tricky. Is a measuring cup more convenient than scales? I think it depends on the country you live in, and the style of recipes you grow accustomed to in magazines, newspapers and cookbooks. A cup is a more convenient way of measuring to me, even though I have scales out on the kitchen bench. But it's never an accurate way of measuring. One cup of cherry tomatoes can weigh between 150g and 200g, depending on the size of the tomatoes. A loosely packed cup of flour will drop in volume if tapped. But a cup is something that most people can visualise and a gram weight is more difficult, although you can buy most things already weighed or measured. I've tried to put in both measurements, and occasionally listed things by count (3 small potatoes, for instance), and I've used tablespoon measures often, because I think it is easier. However, my recommendation when baking is to use scales. (Australian readers take note that a tablespoon measures 15ml in NZ, SA, USA and UK, while in Australia it measures 20ml.)

You'll notice some discrepancies with herbs and salad leaves. These ingredients vary depending on the amount of stalk to leaf. Quite frankly, it doesn't matter if you use a bit more or a bit less.

Salt

When those little dishes of sparkly Maldon sea salt crystals started appearing on restaurant tables, it was hard to resist putting one's fingers in the bowl and running the flakes through them. It was a sensuous experience not to be missed, and salt was added to food whether it needed it or not, just for the pleasure of playing with it.

Once we had fallen in love with Maldon, we were ready for an assault of the olfactory glands and taste buds. Along came Fleur de Sel from the Carmargue, Sel de Guérande from Brittany, Ravidà salt from the western coast of Sicily, and organic and macrobiotic salts, and grey salts, pink salts, orange salts and red salts. Some smell like rotten eggs and taste even worse, but others smell of the fresh sea, vaguely floral or lemony, herbaceous, or of oysters and seaweed, fishing rope and rockpools. It's easy to get hooked. The trouble is, very few of these salts (Ravidà is an exception and there may be others) naturally contain iodine, and fewer still have it added. Without iodine in our diets, humans suffer from goitre and its side effects. For this reason, many countries force salt producers to add iodine to their product. It seems to have been an effective way of getting iodine to the masses but I'm not qualified to comment on the rights or wrongs of this worldwide practice.

I reckon the way around this conundrum – a sort of way having your cake and eating it too – is to use the delicious crunchy flakes of sea salt where you can see, smell and taste the difference (and paying heaps for them makes it worthwhile), and use iodised salt, which usually sells for a fraction of the price of the trendier salts, in cooking and baking.

Hot tips

- Keep seafood refrigerated until just prior to cooking because every hour it is held at room temperature is equivalent to 24 hours of refrigerated life. If shopping for seafood on a hot day, or if you're not able to get it to a refrigerator quickly, take a chilled container with you and keep the seafood in it until you get home.

- Thaw frozen meat slowly in the refrigerator because there will be less moisture loss, meaning more succulent meat. Thaw bulkier seafood in the same way, but thaw small shellfish quickly under running cold water.

- Bring meat to room temperature before cooking because the denser parts may be very chilled, slowing down cooking. This is particularly important for poultry and large cuts of meat.

- Chilling reduces the flavour of food. If serving a dish straight from the freezer (gazpacho, for instance), it may need more seasoning once chilled. If reheating a dish, check it for seasoning once it is heated.

Good stuff

WHILE food rules change frequently, some things remain constant: we should eat less red meat, animal fat, refined carbohydrates and sugar, and more fish, vegetables and fruit. And we should take more exercise.

There's a lot of talk about antioxidants and free radicals in this book, and there are some other long-winded words. Don't be put off – they're only words. All you need to remember is that antioxidants are good and that the only time it was good being free and radical was at university. Think of the good guys (antioxidants) and bad guys (free radicals), and that every day your body has a war raging inside it with all the food and liquid you ingest, and the pollution, chemicals and toxins that make their way, often insidiously, inside you. You must ensure that the good guys win the battle, every day. You do that simply by eating enough food rich in antioxidants to ensure the free radicals and their mates are quashed. Think of it as a game, but a game you must always win.

The most restrictive thing about eating well is the limitations you set yourself. Rather than drawing up a list of 'can't haves', think instead of the 'can haves'. There is a huge range of food rich in antioxidants – you needn't be restricted to a diet of things you don't enjoy. But there's a lot of damaging food out there that you might need to wean yourself off to maintain the balance of a healthy diet. It is never too late to alter the composition of your internal 'chemical soup', to change it from a toxic one to a healthful one. You just have to know how to do it, and be inspired to do it. With knowledge, eating properly becomes second nature. Food as medicine, when it tastes good, is a delight to swallow!

Free-loaders and party-poopers

Free radicals are like free-loaders at a party. No one really invited them, but they got through the door and now they're looking for someone to hitch up with. The thing is, they're no good on their own, and unless they get a date pretty quickly, they'll fade into the shadows and never be seen again.

Free radicals latch onto the nearest molecule; they're not fussy. Then they start their attack, eventually destroying the DNA of the cell they attached themselves to. The damaged cell can then replicate itself with serious consequences.

Free radicals may cause cardiovascular disease, heart disease, cancer, and much more. They're a serious threat to good health and long life – oh yes, they're responsible for premature aging too!

It's impossible to avoid free radicals, as the body produces them as it creates energy. They are also formed through stress and illness, and we absorb them through sunlight and radiation (X-rays), pollution and smoking (including passive smoking). But a lot come via what we ingest, and that's perhaps the easiest part for us to control.

Free radicals are present in fried foods (foods you buy as well as food you fry at home), some refined foods (commercially made biscuits, cakes, puddings, crackers, white bread), snack foods such as potato crisps, and margarine or hydrogenated products, food preservatives and peroxides, among other things.

Fortunately, the body has its own weaponry (antioxidants) to kill off the bad guys, and it does a pretty smart job of it – back to the party analogy, they're like your parents coming in and telling you the party's over. Antioxidants neutralise free radicals and stop them damaging our bodies.

But it's always a delicate balance, and any of those factors mentioned (stress, illness, pollution, bad diet, smoking, etc) can upset the system.

Antioxidants are to be found in abundance in fresh fruit and vegetables, dried fruits, herbs, garlic, chillies, ginger, cereals, wholemeal or wholegrain bread, nuts, seeds, pulses, seafood – especially oily deep water fish, extra virgin olive oil, dark chocolate and cocoa, coffee, tea, beer, fruit juice, red wine and white wine (less than in red wine) and much more.

In other words, you can still have a party but you get to choose who you invite!

The most common antioxidants in food are: vitamin C (in fruit and vegetables); vitamin E (in nuts, whole grains and vegetable oils such as olive oil and avocado); carotenoids, such as beta-carotene (in orange and yellow fruit and vegetables, and green vegetables) and lycopene (in tomatoes); flavonoids and phenolic acids (in fruit and vegetables, chocolate, tea, red wine and red grapes); and sulphur compounds (in garlic, onions, broccoli and Brussels sprouts).

Eat your coloureds

No longer should we say 'eat your greens'. Part of the balancing act is eating greens (broccoli, cabbage), reds (berries, plums), purples (red cabbage, aubergine), and oranges/yellows (carrots, persimmons).

Fruits and vegetables that are coloured all the way through, such as blueberries and beetroot, rather than just on the skin, such as apple, are better for you because they contain more antioxidants.

Health tips

- Try to eat the skin of fruits and vegetables if possible, i.e. apple skins, because they contain antioxidants.

- Use olive oil rather than butter in cooking.

- If you drink tea made from tea leaves, have it in between meals, not with food (drinking tea with a meal will interfere with iron absorption from plant foods).

- Use herbs, nuts and seeds to provide a range of nutrients.

- Make big pots of homemade soup with a variety of vegetables.

- Whenever possible, steam vegetables rather than boiling them, to retain the water-soluble antioxidants such as vitamin C.

- Amazingly, processing, freezing and canning often improve the level of goodness in some foods because the antioxidants are released and we can more easily absorb them (for example, carotenoids found in tomato paste or canned tomatoes have more available lycopene than those in fresh tomatoes).

beach days

Roasted Asparagus and Tomatoes with Hazelnut Dressing

8 vine-ripened plum tomatoes

caster sugar

sea salt to taste

freshly ground black pepper to taste

extra virgin olive oil

750–900g plump asparagus (20 spears)

3 tablespoons hazelnut oil

1 tablespoon creamy Dijonnaise mustard

1 tablespoon lemon juice

250g feta cheese of your choice

60g (3 cups, tightly packed) trimmed
    rocket leaves

20g (1 cup) fresh mint leaves

SERVES 4

HALVE the tomatoes lengthways and put them in a shallow oiled oven tray (I use a Swiss roll tin lined with baking paper to make cleaning easier). Sprinkle with caster sugar, sea salt and black pepper, then drizzle with a little extra virgin olive oil. Roast in an oven preheated to 210°C (fanbake) for 12–15 minutes, or until the tomatoes are collapsing and caramelising around the edges.

Trim the asparagus spears and put them in a shallow ovenproof dish. Drizzle with extra virgin olive oil and season with a little salt and black pepper. Cook for about 20 minutes in the hot oven until they have coloured on the stems and caramelised on the tips.

Mix the hazelnut oil with $3/4$ teaspoon of salt, and add the mustard, black pepper to taste and lemon juice. Whisk until thick.

Cut the feta into eight slices. Put the rocket and mint in a bowl, whisk the dressing again and pour half of it over the salad. Toss the salad well and put some on each plate along with the asparagus, feta and tomatoes. Drizzle the rest of the dressing over.

Titbits

These tomatoes are so delicious and keep so well that you might as well do a big tray of them while you've got the oven on. They're more sharply flavoured than the slow-roasted tomatoes used in other recipes in this book. The asparagus, too, is just irresistible – if you pinch a spear while you're assembling the dish, you won't be able to stop eating them! If you like hazelnuts, add some to this salad (toasted, skinned and chopped).

Pick up

I like a firm ewe's milk feta marinated in olive oil and mint for this dish. Buy big, plump, erect asparagus spears because they remain wonderfully juicy in the centre while the outside turns gloriously crisp. Did you know there are male and female asparagus plants? The male plants produce more spears and live longer, but the female plants produce the fattest, juiciest spears. Wouldn't you know it?

Essential

Exquisite oil. If you can't find or afford hazelnut oil – and it is a treat – use the best extra virgin olive oil you can find. If you are shelling out for expensive oil, make sure you buy it from a supplier with a fast turnover as it is likely to be fresher. Avoid buying oils in clear glass bottles that are stored in sunlight – most oils are sensitive to light and heat, and they quickly go rancid.

Alongside

This could be served with crusty bread as a lunch dish, or a starter followed by grilled or barbecued fish, perhaps rubbed with roasted ground cumin (see Souvlakia, page 43) and drizzled with olive oil. Accompany with rice, couscous or burghul. This is definitely sauvignon blanc territory.

Up front

The tomatoes can be cooked several days in advance.

X-Factor

Stop worrying about the fat content of nuts – most of it is unsaturated, and in hazelnuts most of it is monounsaturated (even better). Think instead of the other goodies they bring to the diet – B vitamins and vitamin E, folate and other minerals.

Asparagus contains a generous collection of vitamins from the A, B and C groups, along with plenty of potassium, good amounts of calcium, magnesium and phosphorous. It also has good quantities of folic acid and rutin (an antioxidant). It has practically no fat, contains some fibre and is low in calories. There is also plenty of vitamin C and lycopene from the tomatoes, and there are nutrients from the greens in this healthy salad.

Crispy Crumbed Prawns

16 green king prawns (if frozen, thaw
  slowly in the refrigerator)
4 tablespoons (¼ cup) fine dry
  breadcrumbs
1 large clove garlic, crushed
1 tablespoon finely chopped flat-leafed
  parsley
a few pinches of salt
4–6 tablespoons olive oil
1 tablespoon lemon juice

SERVES 4

PREPARE the prawns first. Twist off the heads, then peel off the shells, leaving the small piece of shell on the tail intact. Slit down the back of each prawn with a sharp knife and gently extract the black or orangey-red vein running lengthways. Rinse and pat dry with absorbent kitchen paper.

In a shallow dish, mix the breadcrumbs, garlic, parsley and salt, then work in 4 tablespoons of the oil and the lemon juice. The mixture should not be too stiff so add a little extra oil if necessary. Add the prawns to the dish and bury them in the breadcrumb mixture. Leave them for 15–20 minutes.

Choose flat-edged skewers (not rounded ones, as the prawns would flop around on them). Oil them lightly, then put 3 or 4 prawns on each skewer by curling them up and piercing them twice with the skewer. Pat on the breadcrumb mixture. (At first it might seem impossible to get the crumbs to stick, but press the mixture firmly – it will adhere with force!).

Cook the prawns over a medium to hot barbecue for 1–2 minutes; you'll see them change to a pinky-coral colour. Turn and cook the second side until just cooked through. Serve hot.

Titbits

Hungry men (and women) have been known to fall to their knees salivating and begging me for more of these succulent morsels. Alas, it's true, you can never make enough of these expensive little devils. Fill them up on bread first, is one option. Ban kids is another. But maybe the third is the best – serve them only to your lover, by candlelight, and watch the prawns do their magic!

Pick up

If you're paying top dollar, you want prawns with their own passport – you know where they're going, but you need to know where they've come from! They need to be in mint condition. Thawing frozen prawns slowly in the refrigerator, instead of on the worktop in a warm kitchen, prevents moisture loss, so you can be sure they'll be tender and succulent. Look for flat-edged skewers and, when you find some, treat yourself to a dozen of them so they'll be ready and waiting for the day you feel like having a prawn extravaganza.

Essential

A lover, if that's your plan. Otherwise, if serving to a big group, you need a big bank balance to match.

Alongside

Stick to seafood. You could quite happily serve an elegant champagne with these prawns, or a pinot gris or a light, lemony chardonnay.

Up front

Thaw and peel the prawns ahead. Have the breadcrumbs on hand.

X-Factor

Yes, prawns are good for you – they have vitamin B12, niacin, calcium, phosphorous, iodine, selenium, that sort of stuff.

Scampi with Piquillo Peppers

1kg (about 18) scampi (if frozen, thaw
slowly in the refrigerator)

1 tablespoon olive oil

225g jar Spanish piquillo peppers, drained
but reserve the juice

1 small vine-ripened tomato, quartered,
deseeded and diced

3 large green olives, diced, stones
discarded

lemon-infused extra virgin olive oil or
extra virgin olive oil

1 lemon, cut into eighths, for squeezing
over peppers (optional)

SERVES 8 AS A TAPA

PREPARE the scampi first. Twist off the heads, then use small pointed scissors to snip both sides of the soft under-shell of the scampi. Fold back the under-shell to reveal the scampi meat, then detach it from the main shell. Gently pull out the blackish-red vein. Rinse and pat dry with absorbent kitchen paper.

Put the olive oil in a frying pan and set it over a medium heat. When heated, add the prepared scampi. Cook gently for a couple of minutes each side or until just cooked. Transfer to a plate.

Cut each piece of piquillo pepper in half through the folded sides and flick out any seeds. Curl a piece of pepper around each scampi. Arrange on a serving platter. Garnish with the diced tomato and green olives and drizzle with a little lemon-infused olive oil. Serve with lemon wedges for squeezing over if using.

Titbits

These tapas are so delectable, when you serve them you'll be wishing you'd made more of them – until you remember the sore fingers you're nursing, (pricked by the scampi shells). You could pay more for the scampi and buy them already shelled. They're a knife-and-fork job to eat, rather than eat-in-the-fingers tapas.

Essential

Spanish piquillo peppers – these are exquisite little morsels in their own right, but there's a lot you can do with them. The small red peppers, shaped like a pointed bird's beak, are smoked over oak, then skinned and bottled in their own sweet juices. Don't waste the juices – add them to dressings.

Alongside

As part of a selection of tapas, these scampi will stand out. They're delicate, so serve them first. You could also serve this dish as a starter for four people, and follow with a seafood main course. Sauvignon blanc will go adorably with the peppers, even more so if it has been aged in oak.

Up front

If you've got scampi to shell, the motto is 'sooner rather than later'. The scampi will keep quite happily, covered and refrigerated, for up to 24 hours providing they were absolutely fresh when you bought them, or freshly thawed.

X-Factor

This is nutritionally a good bet! You've got B vitamins, selenium, calcium, phosphorous and copper in the scampi, vitamins A, B and C in the peppers, and a few extra important bits and bobs in the tomatoes, olives, olive oil and lemon.

Feta Salad with Pickled Red Onions

PUT the white vinegar in a saucepan with the water, the sugar and a few pinches of sea salt. Add the sliced onion and bring slowly to the boil. As soon as the liquid is boiling, turn off the heat. Leave the onion in the liquid for 5 minutes, then drain.

Arrange the cos lettuce leaves in a serving bowl. Break the feta into large crumbly pieces and pat dry with absorbent kitchen paper. Put the feta on top of the lettuce. In a small bowl mix the olive oil, lemon juice and garlic with black pepper to taste and a few pinches of sea salt. Rub the oregano between the palms of your hands to release the fragrance and flavour, and scatter over the salad. Add the olives and top everything with the pickled red onion. Remix the dressing and pour over the salad.

125ml (¹/₂ cup) white vinegar
250ml (1 cup) water
1 teaspoon white sugar
sea salt
1 large red onion, sliced into thin wedges
1 small cos lettuce, broken into leaves, washed and dried
200g feta cheese
3 tablespoons extra virgin olive oil
1 tablespoon lemon juice
1 clove garlic, crushed
freshly ground black pepper to taste
1 teaspoon dried oregano
¹/₄ cup small black olives, drained

SERVES 6 AS A STARTER

Titbits

A simple, effective use of ingredients which when they're combined smell and taste of summer.

Pick up

Firm feta – I don't like soft, squishy feta and think a firmer type is better in salads such as this.
Greek or Sicilian dried oregano, if you can find it – it is much more aromatic.

Essential

Good bread to serve with the salad.

Alongside

Serve with a loaf of decent bread.
An oak-aged sauvignon blanc will be perfect with the feta, or try a white rioja.

Up front

The onion can be pickled, the feta crumbled, the cos lettuce washed and dried, and the dressing ingredients prepared an hour or two in advance.

X-Factor

Onions are a goodie – they contain antioxidants and are good for the blood – as is garlic, which is a natural antibiotic and an antifungal. Feta cheese contains vitamin B12, calcium and phosphorous. Extra virgin olive oil, olives, lemon juice and lettuce add up to giving this starter a big health tick.

Spaghetti with Rocket and Capers

PUT the capers in a sieve, then rinse well under running water. Soak in fresh water for 30 minutes, then drain and rinse again.

Heat 2 tablespoons of the extra virgin olive oil in a small frying pan and when hot add the breadcrumbs. Cook until they are golden and crisp, turning them often. Transfer to a side plate.

Cook the pasta in plenty of gently boiling, well-salted water until al dente.

While the pasta is cooking, peel the garlic and chop it very finely. Put the rest of the olive oil in a small pan, add the garlic and chillies and warm gently over a low heat, so the garlic and chillies flavour the oil; don't let the garlic fry.

Drain the pasta and transfer to a large heated serving bowl. Quickly add the lemon zest and capers to the oil, then pour it over the pasta. Toss well, then add the rocket and basil. Toss carefully, scatter the breadcrumbs over, then serve with parmesan cheese.

4 tablespoons ($1/4$ cup) salted capers
150ml extra virgin olive oil
30g ($1/2$ cup) fresh white breadcrumbs
500g spaghetti
salt
2 cloves garlic
2 tiny dried 'bird's eye' chillies, crushed
finely grated zest of 1 lemon
80g (4 cups, tightly packed) trimmed rocket leaves
30g (1 cup) small basil leaves
freshly grated parmesan (parmigiano reggiano) cheese for serving

SERVES 4-6 AS A STARTER OR 3-4 AS A LIGHT MEAL

Titbits

Olive oil is an integral part of this sauce, used because it is nutritious, delicious and acts as a carrier for the other flavourings. If you cut back the oil, the sauce will be tacky.

Pick up

'Bird's eye' chillies. These are small, dried, hot chillies, the best substitute for the chilli used in Italy. They are tongue tinglers as opposed to throat burners.

Alongside

This makes a tasty starter to precede a light main course. On a night when you're not up to much cooking but you crave a whack of flavour, serve it as a main course, accompanied by a tomato and basil salad dressed with a squirt of lemon, a few flakes of sea salt and a smattering of freshly ground black pepper.
A few chunks of crunchy bread (ciabatta heated in the oven) won't go astray with this pasta dish. An oak-aged sauvignon blanc should have enough character to stand up to these flavours.

Up front

None to do – this is one of those dishes where you put the water on to boil and cook the pasta, by which time the sauce is ready, the table is set and you've poured yourself a glass of wine to boot.

X-Factor

No kidding, this dish is good for you! Garlic keeps you healthy, parmesan is an easily digested low-fat source of protein, pasta slowly releases its energy over a period of time (it's good fuel), and rocket has a range of minerals. Extra virgin olive oil is fat, yes, and it's high in calories, but most of the fat is monounsaturated and it is a great source of the antioxidant vitamin E.

Chicken Breasts with Rosemary and Garlic

4 single chicken breasts, skin and fat
    removed
4 tablespoons plain flour
3 tablespoons olive oil
2–3 tablespoons butter
salt to taste
freshly ground black pepper to taste
4 cloves garlic, finely chopped
2 tablespoons chopped rosemary
125ml (1/2 cup) dry white wine or chicken
    stock

SERVES 4

CUT each chicken breast into three pieces of even thickness (cut off the tail-end as one piece, then slit the other piece through the middle). Coat the pieces with flour, dusting off the excess.

Set a frying pan over a medium heat. When hot add 2 tablespoons of olive oil, then a good knob of butter. Put in the pieces of chicken while the butter is sizzling. Cook the pieces of chicken for about 5 minutes a side, or until golden and cooked through.

Transfer the chicken pieces to a heated plate when done. If you need to cook the chicken in two batches, keep the first lot warm in a heated oven, then add another tablespoon of oil to the pan and cook the remaining chicken pieces in the same way. When all the chicken is cooked, season it with salt and black pepper.

If the pan is dry, add a knob of butter, then drop in the garlic and rosemary. Cook for a few minutes until the garlic is just starting to colour, then return the chicken pieces to the pan. Turn them over in the garlic and rosemary butter, then tip all the contents of the pan onto a heated serving platter. Let the pan cool for a few minutes, then pour in the white wine. Let it bubble for a few minutes, then pour it over the chicken and serve immediately.

Titbits

Rosemary and garlic were made for each other and whenever they cosy-up together in the pan the result is mouthwateringly good. This is easy enough to do for a family summer's meal, but because it tastes so good you needn't feel shy about dishing it up to the most discerning guests.

Pick up

If you don't have any rosemary growing in your garden, make sure what you buy is supple and not dry and medicinal-smelling.

Essential

Good quality chicken breasts. A lot of pre-packaged chicken breasts are hideously large and pumped full of water. There's only one way to go and that's free-range corn-fed and organic.

Alongside

For the family, serve with a good tasty green salad of mixed leaves and a loaf of crunchy bread. For guests, serve with crunchy spuds of some sort, or kumara (sweet potatoes), baked mushrooms and green beans. The gutsy flavours of rosemary and garlic ensure this dish can take quite a big chardonnay.

Up front

The chicken can be cut into pieces well ahead of time; keep it covered and refrigerated until ready to cook. The garlic can be peeled ahead, too, but don't chop it or the rosemary until just before using because the garlic loses potency and the rosemary darkens in colour.

X-Factor

Getting rid of the chicken skin gets rid of a lot of fat. It's a pity we have to put some back in to make the dish taste great (there's nothing wrong with steamed chicken, but this is not a steamed dish!).

Glazed Ham with Palm Sugar and Kaffir Lime Leaves

CUT a scallop pattern around the shank end of the ham skin. Working from there, remove the ham's skin, using your fingers to ease it away from the fat (try not to disturb the layer of creamy fat). Using a sharp knife, score diamond shapes into the fat, but don't cut into the meat. Put the ham in a large roasting tin. Combine the rest of the ingredients, except for the star anise, and spoon these over the ham, then arrange the star anise on top.

Bake in an oven preheated to 150°C (fanbake) for 2 hours. Every 15 minutes, scoop up the glaze and baste the ham with it. At the end of this time, the ham will be beautifully golden brown and will be warmed right through. The ham will also cook superbly in a covered kettle barbecue, though be careful to keep the temperature low.

1 whole leg of ham on the bone, cooked
160g (1 cup) crushed palm sugar
2 tablespoons ginger juice (grate the ginger and squeeze out the juice)
2 tablespoons crushed garlic
1 kaffir lime leaf, finely shredded
2 tablespoons lime juice
1 mild red chilli, deseeded and finely chopped
1 teaspoon five spice powder
whole star anise

Titbits

If a ham is well done, I think it is a magnificent thing because it feeds so many, isn't difficult to slice, can be served hot or cold, and there's always plenty left over for sandwiches or fry-ups the next day. Thick chunks of ham off the bone sizzled in butter are to die for!

This is a stunning way to glaze a cooked ham on the bone. The palm sugar (available at Asian food stores) forms a crunchy topping and, providing the temperature doesn't get too high, it forms a gorgeous golden glaze. You will probably need to grate or chop the palm sugar with a large sharp knife.

A good tip to keep the roasting tin clean is to line it with a double thickness of heavy-duty aluminium foil, bringing it right the way up the sides of the tin. When the ham is cooked, the foil can be removed and discarded and the roasting tin will be as clean as a whistle.

Leftover ham will store for more than a week providing it is not kept at room temperature for any length of time (slice it, rewrap it and refrigerate it). And remember not to store a ham for long in plastic — it has to be able to breathe. Wrap it loosely with waxed paper to protect the glaze, then store it in a dish large enough to contain it, or in a muslin ham bag (these are sold in kitchen stores), or wrapped loosely in clean muslin.

I'm of the opinion that it is easier to carve a ham down to the bone than across the bone. Start with the shank on your left (reverse this if you're left-handed) and make a vertical cut down to the bone, then another one slightly on the right of it and lever out the slice.

Continue slicing this way as far as you can, then start on the left-hand side. Slicing a ham like this gives beautiful neat slices, each with a little of the fat and delicious glaze.

A knife with a long, thin blade is the best for slicing ham.

Freeze the bone and little chunks of meat taken off the bone separately, until you have time to make stock — this is the base for a fabulous pea and ham soup (see page 127).

Essential

It's the blend of ingredients that creates this magic taste — you can't leave anything out!

Alongside

A whole ham by its nature is suited for special occasions because it serves so many people — a medium-sized ham serves around 50 as part of a buffet meal. Emphasise the flavourings and serve Asian salads and noodle dishes with it. You could go for a pinot noir or red rioja to accompany the ham, or keep things light and match the spice with a chenin blanc, colombard, or gewürztraminer.

Up front

The ham can be served hot, or it can be left to cool down, then served warmish, or cold.

X-Factor

There are plenty of B group vitamins in ham, but unfortunately quite a lot of sodium is used in the curing process. Eat in small quantities and enjoy it when you do.

Gazpacho Shooters

1 small red onion

1 slice stale, coarse-textured bread, without too much crust

1 medium telegraph cucumber (long, tender-skinned cucumber)

400g can tomatoes (Spanish or Italian)

2 large cloves garlic, chopped (remove any greenish sprouts)

1 teaspoon smoked hot Spanish paprika

$1\frac{1}{4}$ teaspoons salt

$1\frac{1}{2}$ tablespoons extra virgin olive oil

1 medium red pepper (capsicum), halved, deseeded, cored and finely chopped

2 tablespoons Spanish sherry or red wine vinegar

2 tablespoons Tio Pepe or dry sherry (optional)

chilled water

MAKES ABOUT 800ML – ALLOW AROUND 50ML A SHOT (16 SINGLE SHOTS, OR 8 DOUBLES)

SLICE the onion finely, put it in a bowl, pour on cold water to cover and soak for 15 minutes.

Put the bread slice in a shallow dish, cover with cold water and soak for 15 minutes.

Peel the cucumber, then cut lengthways and scoop out the seeds with a teaspoon. Chop the flesh coarsely.

Put the tomatoes in a bowl and scoop out as many seeds as possible (easily done with a small teaspoon).

Drain the onion and put it in the bowl of a food processor with the garlic, smoked paprika, salt and olive oil. Squeeze the excess water out of the bread and add to the processor bowl. Blend until smooth. Add the red pepper and sherry or red wine vinegar and blend again until smooth. Add the cucumber and tomatoes and process until very smooth. Pass the soup through a sieve set over a bowl and stir in $\frac{1}{2}$ cup of chilled water if necessary to achieve pouring consistency.

Chill the gazpacho for several hours, then check the seasoning – it may need more salt or vinegar. About 45 minutes before serving, put the gazpacho in the freezer; leave until it is forming icy shards around the sides of the bowl. Whisk the second measure of sherry through, if using. Serve icy cold, ladled into small chilled shot glasses.

Titbits

Icy cold slugs of gazpacho taken on a sultry evening send a welcome shiver down the spine. When I say icy shards, that's what I mean – it should be arrestingly cold.

Add a layer of deep, smoky intrigue with a dash of Spanish paprika and a splash of Tio Pepe and enjoy the wafting spicy floral scents – the epitome of summer!

I use a well-trimmed chunk of sour dough bread because I like the hint of sourness it gives, but any well-made white bread will do.

Pick up

Smoked Spanish paprika. If you can't get it, don't use the faded dull red stuff in the back of your pantry – you'll be adding musty, dusty red powder instead of vibrant, smoky red pepper intrigue.

Essential

Good tomatoes. I've recommended canned tomatoes to be sure the result will be as it should be, but if you happen to have superb vine-ripened full-flavoured tomatoes, then use them.

Alongside

A swig of this serves the same purpose as a blast from a fan up your shirt or skirt on a hot, sticky night. It's not meant to be a meal, just a chill thrill to cool you down. Serve whatever you want after, but it does lead rather nicely on to a full Spanish repast, or a feast of tapas.

Up front

The whole lot can be prepared in advance, except hold back the Tio Pepe until serving time, then splash it in, swirl it around and pour into chilled glasses. Serve immediately. The Tio Pepe should also be on ice.

X-Factor

This is goodness in a glass – not only does it invigorate, but it's a real tonic for the body (phytochemicals, antioxidants, sulphides, flavonoids and natural antibiotics).

Green Tomato Salad with Fried Fish, Avocado and Orange

HAVE everything out on the worktop and ready to go before cooking the fish.

Heat the olive oil in a large frying pan over a high heat until it is very hot. Coat half the pieces of fish with flour, dusting off excess, then put them in the hot oil. Cook quickly until golden, then turn and cook the second side until only just cooked through.

While the fish is cooking, slice the green and red tomatoes and put them on a large platter. Scatter the garlic on, squeeze the limes over and season with salt and pepper.

As the fish is cooked, transfer it to the platter, arranging it on top of the tomatoes. Sprinkle lightly with salt. Continue with the rest of the fish.

When all the fish is cooked, put the orange slices and avocado on top and sprinkle the coriander over. Drizzle with a little lemon-infused extra virgin olive oil, then sprinkle the chilli and olives on top. Serve immediately.

100ml olive oil

1kg small skinned and boned white fish fillets, rinsed, patted dry and cut into thirds

60g (1/2 cup) plain flour

2 large green tomatoes

2 large vine-ripened tomatoes

3 cloves young garlic, finely chopped

juice of 2 limes

sea salt

freshly ground black pepper to taste

2 juicy oranges, peeled and thinly sliced

2 ripe but firm avocados, peeled, stoned and sliced

2 tablespoons chopped coriander

lemon-infused extra virgin olive oil

2 fresh hot red chillies, halved, deseeded and chopped

60g (1/4 cup) tiny black olives

SERVES 6

Titbits

This is sensational and perfect for outdoor summer eating, day or night, the quintessential *Hot Nights, Cool Days* dish! It's all about balance of smells, colours, tastes and textures, like sniffing the sea and biting off a big chunk of sunshine!

Pick up

Buy juicy oranges and firm, not squishy, avocados. When using garlic raw, look for taut white bulbs and cloves with no soft spots or green sprouting showing (yellowing cloves will be rank). If the garlic has started to sprout, split each clove in half with a sharp knife and pick out the centre sprout (it's the bit that repeats on you later!). If you can afford it, buy lemon-infused olive oil. Otherwise, use extra virgin olive oil.

Essential

The green tomatoes add texture and acidity – don't leave them out! Fresh juicy limes – their perfume mixed with chilli, garlic, oranges and coriander is just magical.

Alongside

Make a fabulous rice salad with warm jasmine rice tossed with a few shallots (eschallots) and a little chopped garlic sizzled in butter until lightly golden. Add a few plump raisins and top the rice with flaked almonds sizzled in a little butter until golden.
To drink with it I'd opt for a chardonnay with citrus tones and one with a creamy mouth-feel to help draw in the voluptuous texture of the avocado.

Up front

Prepare the fish, but keep it refrigerated (every hour seafood is kept at room temperature is equivalent to 24 hours of refrigerated life). Peel the oranges and keep them refrigerated. Weigh and sort out the ingredients, but peel and chop them as you cook the fish.

X-Factor

Yes, this has it – fish is brain food! Tomatoes contain lycopene. Garlic is a life-giver and citrus contains antioxidants. And the avocado is an exceptional fruit, containing more protein and fat than any other fruit, but the fat is mostly monounsaturated. Nutritional experts have labelled the avocado 'nutrient-dense', which means it provides at least four essential nutrients in the same percentage as the calories it supplies. Avocados provide five essential nutrients in this proportion: vitamins A, B6, C, folic acid and the mineral copper. They are a good source of energy, are easily digested (making them suitable for babies), and their high protein content makes them a valuable food for vegetarians. Half an avocado provides about the same amount of calories as 25g (2 1/2 tablespoons) butter (180 calories), and can be used as a spread on bread or toast in place of butter.

Panfried Peaches with Roasted Chicken and Crispy Tarragon

RINSE the chicken inside and out, removing any lumps of fat. Drain, then pat dry with absorbent kitchen paper. Put a nut of butter inside the chicken, along with a sprig of tarragon and a little salt and black pepper. Slip some tarragon sprigs between the chicken breast skin and meat. Tie the chicken legs together with string, hooking the string around the parson's nose to keep the cavity closed. Then put the chicken, breast uppermost, in a smallish roasting tin, choosing one in which it fits snugly. Pour the chicken stock in.

Melt 25g of butter and brush over the chicken. Squeeze on a little lemon juice and sprinkle with salt. Put the chicken in an oven preheated to 180°C (regular) and cook for about 1½ hours, basting often (turn the chicken over after 20 minutes, cook for a further 20 minutes, then turn breast uppermost again for the rest of the cooking). The chicken should be kept moist during cooking; add more stock if it dries up. Halfway through cooking, or when you turn the chicken breast up again, strew the chicken generously with plenty of tarragon sprigs which will turn deliciously crisp.

Remove the chicken from the oven when it is cooked through to the bone and let it rest at room temperature for 1½–2 hours, covered with a ventilated cover, keeping the tarragon on a separate plate to keep it crisp.

Cut the peppers in half, remove the cores and seeds and cut into chunks. Heat the olive oil in a medium frying pan and when it is hot add the peppers. Cook for about 10 minutes, turning the peppers, until they are just starting to wilt. Transfer them to a dish.

Have the chicken ready, cut into joints and arranged on a large platter.

Slice the peaches into thick wedges. Heat a large frying pan over a medium heat, and when it is hot drop in a knob of butter. Add the peach wedges while the butter is sizzling and cook for about 3 minutes each side, turning carefully. Add the peppers, season with salt and black pepper and pour everything, juices too, over the chicken. Strew the top with basil, toss lightly, then break the pieces of crispy tarragon over the top. Serve immediately.

1 free-range corn-fed organic chicken, 1.3–1.4kg
butter
generous handful of fresh tarragon
salt to taste
freshly ground black pepper to taste
250ml (1 cup) chicken stock (more if needed)
1½ lemons
2 yellow peppers (capsicums)
2 tablespoons extra virgin olive oil
3 firm late-season peaches
fresh basil leaves for serving

SERVES 6

Titbits

Peaches are a great summertime treat – teeth sinking into flesh that just gives way, sweet juice dribbling down the chin and wrist, and that irresistible fruity peach fragrance wafting around. If you think a peach is just a peach, think again: hot pan, sizzling butter and frying peaches – roll over Chicken Maryland!

Pick up

Gorgeous peaches! Wait until late summer to make this dish and choose sweet and juicy, golden, firm-fleshed peaches – the type you use for bottling. And pick up a bottle of fruity gewürztraminer, which will be heavenly with the peaches, or match exotic with exotic, and buy an opulent viognier.

Essential

Fresh tarragon – and it must be the French variety.

Alongside

The chicken is fabulous on its own – but so are the peaches. They're just dynamite served with soft creamy curls of prosciutto (or crispy bacon), drizzled with balsamic vinegar, or drizzled with a little mandarin or lemon-infused olive oil and served with seafood (exquisite), or sprinkled with chopped red chillies and drizzled with lime juice (sensational with quail, duck, chicken, scallops, prawns, crayfish – you could also add shredded kaffir lime leaves or lemon leaves), or served on fried or barbecued fish fillets with a sprinkling of capers and marjoram. Do you know, once you step outside the square (peach as a fruit, in a bottle, as a chutney, or à la Maryland), the possibilities are positively thrilling.

Up front

The chicken can be prepared several hours before cooking. Keep it covered and refrigerated, but bring it to room temperature before cooking. The peppers can be done an hour or so ahead, and the peaches fried at the last minute.

X-Factor

Peaches are good for you, chicken is good for you, peppers are good for you. Accentuate the positives and forget about the negatives (butter and those crispy morsels of chicken skin – no way are you throwing those in the bin!).

Panfried Fish Fillets with Tomatoes and Lime

3 tablespoons extra virgin olive oil

1 large onion, sliced

10 small vine-ripened tomatoes, halved

1kg smallish skinned and boned white fish fillets, rinsed and patted dry

45g (1/3 cup) plain flour

100ml olive oil for frying

salt to taste

freshly ground black pepper to taste

3 tablespoons chopped coriander

3 tablespoons chopped mint

juice of 2 limes

SERVES 6

PUT the extra virgin olive oil in a medium frying pan and set over a low to medium heat. Add the onion and cook gently until it is soft and translucent, about 10 minutes. Put the tomatoes on top, cut side down, and cook for another 5 minutes. Turn off the heat.

Cut each fish fillet in half, then into two or three pieces. Coat half the pieces of fish lightly with flour, dusting off the excess. Meanwhile, have the olive oil heating in a large frying pan and when it is really hot add the floured fish. Fry quickly until a good golden colour, then turn and cook the second side, caring less about the colour but making sure that you cook the fish until it is only just approaching being cooked (it will continue to cook as it stands).

Transfer the fish to a large platter as it is cooked, presenting it with the most golden side facing up. Season with salt and black pepper. Cook the second batch of fish in the same way. Spoon the onion and tomatoes over the fish. Sprinkle the herbs over, then squeeze the lime juice on. Serve immediately.

Titbits

This is a good, uncomplicated fish dish with a lovely sweet flavour from onions and tomatoes. A few squirts of lime and a handful of mint and coriander leaves keeps everything in balance.

Pick up

Fresh fish, of course!

Alongside

I love this with a big bowl of fluffy, fragrant rice. That's all it needs – and a glass or two of sauvignon blanc.

Up front

The onion and tomato mixture can be cooked an hour ahead if need be. But the fish should be cooked just before serving.

X-Factor

Go for it! With fish, onions, tomatoes, extra virgin olive oil, herbs and limes this is good for the brain and heart, lowers cholesterol, fights cancer, and keeps away colds.

Spaghetti with Roasted Tomatoes and Lemon Basil

HALVE the tomatoes and put them in a shallow ovenproof tray (I use a non-stick Swiss roll tin) cut side up. Distribute a little sea salt, black pepper and caster sugar over the cut surfaces and drizzle with a little olive oil (about 25ml – if using lemon-infused oil, reserve it for tossing through the pasta). Bake in an oven preheated to 140°C (fanbake) for about 1 hour, or until the tomatoes have collapsed and the juices are syrupy. Cut the tomatoes in half with sharp scissors.

Cook the pasta in plenty of gently boiling, well-salted water until al dente. Toss the rest of the oil through the cooked spaghetti, adding plenty of black pepper, then add the tomatoes with all their juices, and the basil. Toss carefully. Serve immediately with parmesan cheese.

500g small plum tomatoes or vine-ripened tomatoes
sea salt to taste
freshly ground black pepper to taste
caster sugar
125ml (½ cup) extra virgin olive oil
400g spaghetti
salt
1 cup small lemon basil leaves
freshly grated parmesan (parmigiano reggiano) cheese for serving

SERVES 4 AS A STARTER OR 3 AS A LIGHT MEAL

Titbits

This is a quintessential summer pasta dish – a handful of ingredients easily put together – which delivers more than the sum of its parts. For more information on the tomatoes, see Slow-roasted Tomatoes, page 65.

Pick up

If you can't get lemon basil, use ordinary basil.
Accompany the spaghetti with an inexpensive soave that will highlight the lemon notes in the pasta.

Essential

A good extra virgin olive oil – this is essential! To make the dish even more delicious, substitute some of it with lemon-infused extra virgin olive oil (use 50ml lemon-infused oil and 75ml extra virgin).
Good pasta. Go for one of Italy's big selling brands such as Barilla. And, as always, use only parmigiano reggiano.

Up front

The tomatoes can be made up to a week before using. It then takes no more than 5 minutes to put this together.

X-Factor

Tomatoes are a fabulous food. Lycopene, the antioxidant phytochemical they contain, is increased when the tomatoes are cooked. They are also bursting with vitamins C and E and vitamins from the B group. Pasta is a very useful complex carbohydrate. Parmesan cheese contains vitamin B12, is low in calories and high in calcium and phosphorous. And extra virgin olive oil, which is the basis of this sauce, lowers cholesterol and is rich in vitamin E (if you need an excuse to feel good about eating it, concentrate on the fact that it'll keep your skin looking younger).

Watermelon with Greek Feta and Lemon-infused Oil

¹/₂ tablespoon olive oil

5 tablespoons (¹/₄ cup) pumpkin seeds

sea salt

¹/₂ firm red watermelon, chilled

200g Greek feta cheese, drained, dried and crumbled

lemon-infused extra virgin olive oil for drizzling

freshly ground black pepper to taste

SERVES 6

PUT a small frying pan over a medium heat and when warmed, add the oil. When the oil is hot, add the pumpkin seeds. Now watch out! You'll need to cover the pumpkin seeds as they toast because they explode and jump out of the pan, and they can burn your face or hands. Loosely drape a piece of kitchen paper over the top of them, or use a splatter screen, and keep them covered until they stop popping; you will need to poke a spoon in and stir them occasionally. When they are lightly browned, tip them onto a plate, sprinkle with sea salt and leave to cool. When cool, store them airtight if not using immediately.

Cut the watermelon into wedges. Arrange on a plate with the feta cheese. Drizzle with lemon-infused extra virgin olive oil, grind on some black pepper, scatter the pumpkin seeds over and serve immediately.

Titbits

This is unbelievably simple to construct but, more importantly, it is stunning to eat. It's hard to believe until you try it.

Pick up

The watermelon must be firm, not the sort with the texture of cotton wool. Buy good firm feta, not the squishy type, but it can be made from cow's, goat's or ewe's milk.

Essential

Lemon-infused extra virgin olive oil – it makes all the flavours come together.

Alongside

This is the kind of dish which is good to pick at, and it goes with other food which is good to pick at, too, such as olives, slices of chorizo sausage sizzled in the pan until crisp, hummus and pita bread, dolmades, tzatziki (or caçik), dill pickles, slices or chunks of marinated fried aubergine (eggplant), wood-roasted artichokes, steamed mussels with chilli sauce – that sort of thing. An assortment of the above makes a perfect feast to pick and peck at as the sun sets after a glorious day at the beach. I adore it with a chilled beaujolais or rosé, or a pinot gris.

Up front

There's virtually no preparation with this dish. If you are turning it into a feast, everything can be prepared ahead, purchased ready-made, or cooked on the barbecue in front of the guests. A great way to entertain.

X-Factor

You may be surprised to learn that watermelon is not just water (okay, around 90% of it is water!). It contains vitamin C, lycopene, plus significant amounts of phosphorous. Pumpkin seeds with their range of minerals are well worth introducing into salads and vegetable dishes.

Pawpaw and Strawberry Salad

PEEL the pawpaw, cut in half and scoop out the seeds. Cut the pawpaw into small cubes and put in a bowl with the strawberries. Add the other ingredients and mix carefully. Serve the salad on its own or with yoghurt.

Titbits

Yes, serve it after dinner at the beach by all means, but use it as a super-sexy, healthy, night-after replenishing breakfast, too.

Pick up

A pawpaw that is perfectly ripe. This is easier said than done. It must be blemish-free, firmish but yielding and not tinged with green. The strawberries must also be in perfect condition. Never buy strawberries after heavy rain because they will be tasteless – like tomatoes and grapes, they become bloated with the water.

Essential

The ginger – it adds a hot bite that wakes up the palate. Buy it fresh. If you use old, strong ginger, you won't thank me for this recipe!

X-Factor

Pawpaw aids digestion, making this a valuable end to a meal. It also contains carotenoids (a class of antioxidants), which convert to vitamin A. Strawberries contain phytochemicals and a huge whack of vitamin C. Have a double helping.

1 pawpaw (papaya), chilled
300g (2 cups) strawberries, hulled and sliced
1 fresh lime
1 tablespoon caster sugar
4 kaffir lime leaves, shredded very finely
1 small knob young ginger, peeled and finely shredded

SERVES 4-6

Lamb Racks with Lemon and Honey Crust

2 full racks of young lamb weighing about
   450g each, or 4 racks with 4 cutlets each
2 lemons
2 tablespoons scented honey
3 cloves garlic, crushed
1 tablespoon green peppercorns, rinsed,
   drained and dried
1/4 teaspoon smoked sweet Spanish
   paprika
4 tablespoons extra virgin olive oil
freshly ground black pepper to taste
30g (1/2 cup) fresh breadcrumbs
sea salt to taste

Sautéed Lemons
3 lemons
caster sugar
butter
salt

SERVES 4

PREPARE the lamb racks first, removing excess fat and silverskin if necessary.

Remove the peel from the lemons with an old-fashioned grapefruit peeler (the type with a hook that takes the peel off in thick curls), or peel off thick strips with a knife. Put the lemon rind in a bowl with the honey, garlic, green peppercorns, paprika and olive oil, and black pepper to taste. Mix well.

Put the lamb racks in a shallow dish and pour the marinade over them. Leave to marinate for 30 minutes.

Wrap aluminum foil around the lamb bones to prevent them from burning, and spoon the marinade back onto the meaty parts of the racks. Pat the breadcrumbs on. Cook in an oven preheated to 210°C (fanbake) for 15 minutes for pink juicy lamb; don't overcook (allow an extra 5 minutes if you want them a little more cooked). Transfer the racks to a chopping board and sprinkle generously with sea salt. Let them rest for 5–7 minutes, then slice into cutlets. Arrange on a heated platter with all the lemony bits and serve immediately.

To sauté the lemons, cut them into thick slices, dry on absorbent kitchen paper, then dredge with a little caster sugar. Have ready a small frying pan set over a medium-high heat. Drop in a good knob of butter and when sizzling hot add the lemon slices. Cook until golden and sprinkle lightly with salt. Serve hot as a garnish with the lamb racks.

Titbits

This is just gorgeous! If you don't try it, you'll be missing one of the treasures of this book. Usually, one tries to avoid the white pith on the interior of lemon rind, but in this dish it is tempered by the sweetness of the honey and creates a bitter-sweet flavour which is part of the dish's magic.
If the honey is firm, loosen it in a microwave for a few seconds, or in a small bowl immersed in warm water.

Pick up

Fresh New Zealand lamb. I wish, wherever you are in the world, that you could buy this. I'm not biased just because I come from the land of 40 million sheep, but because it is the best in the world. It is fine-grained, sweet and very tender. Failing New Zealand lamb, buy the freshest lamb you can. I buy the racks with the fat removed and peel off the silverskin.

Alongside

Serve with a burghul pilaf, or couscous, and blanched spinach whipped with yoghurt. There are lots of wine choices – try it with a red Navarra from Spain, or fall back on cabernet sauvignon or merlot.

Up front

Make the breadcrumbs. Trim the lamb racks.

X-Factor

One of the attributes of lamb is the sweetness provided by the fat. It's a fine line between removing enough to satisfy the health police, and leaving enough for gustatory pleasure. That aside, lamb has plenty of the B group vitamins and iron. Iron helps carry oxygen to the whole body, including the brain. Serving the lamb with a grain such as burghul or couscous is a smart idea as it helps the body use the iron from the plant foods, so you get a double dose!

Red Pepper and Fish Kebabs

600g skinned and boned white fish fillets,
rinsed and patted dry
1–2 red peppers (capsicums), halved,
cored, deseeded and cut into chunks
2 tablespoons capers, drained
1 teaspoon chopped marjoram
1 teaspoon chopped oregano
1/4 teaspoon salt
freshly ground black pepper to taste
1 clove garlic, crushed
1 small red onion, very finely chopped
2 tablespoons olive oil

SERVES 4

CUT the fish fillets into large chunks and thread onto bamboo skewers with the pieces of red pepper.

In a shallow ovenproof dish, mix the capers, marjoram, oregano, salt, black pepper, garlic, red onion and olive oil. Put the kebabs in the marinade and turn to coat them on all sides. Cover and set aside for 1 hour to marinate.

Preheat the grill until hot. Turn the kebabs over in the marinade, then put the dish under the grill, close to the source of the heat. Grill for about 7 minutes each side, or until the fish is lightly browned but still moist (take care not to overcook it).

Transfer to a serving dish and serve immediately.

Titbits

Lightly charred sweet peppers and a garlicky, herby marinade give these moist and tender fish kebabs loads of flavour.
To prevent the bamboo skewers from catching alight, soak them in water for 30 minutes before using.

Pick up

Look for white fish fillets that will hold together after cooking, not fillets that flake too easily, and opt for medium fillets, not small, slim ones.

Alongside

These are great with steamed rice, couscous or orzo pasta. Try folding a large bunch of trimmed rocket leaves through hot orzo dressed with sea salt, freshly ground black pepper and a tablespoon of extra virgin olive oil, or lemon or mandarin-infused oil, and putting the kebabs on top. Excellent with sauvignon blanc.

Up front

The kebabs can be prepared several hours in advance, providing they are kept covered and refrigerated.

X-Factor

Fish is 'da bomb' (the best). Here the fish pieces are grilled and have just a little oil (the best kind) in the marinade. Peppers are bursting with vitamin C and have plenty of vitamins A and some B group vitamins too. When this dish is teamed with orzo and rocket, you are eating a plate of goodness.

Souvlakia and Cos Salad

PUT the meat in a bowl and work through the crumbled oregano, black pepper to taste, the cumin, the olive oil and the juice and rind of 1 lemon. (Remove the peel from the lemon with an old-fashioned grapefruit peeler – the type with a hook that takes the peel off in thick curls – or peel off thick strips with a knife.) Refrigerate for several hours, turning the meat in the flavourings from time to time.

Thread the meat and vegetables on skewers. Drizzle with a little olive oil and cook on a hot barbecue grill for about 12 minutes, turning frequently. When ready, season with sea salt, transfer to a plate and serve hot with wedges of lemon and Cos Salad (see page 45).

Titbits

Don't use fatty cheap lamb for these kebabs – we're talking fast cooking here so it must be a prime cut, either from the rump or leg. To make it less messy, line a bowl with a clean plastic bag and put the meat in it with the seasoning. Tie the top of the bag then put the bag, still nestled inside the bowl, in the refrigerator. It's easy to turn the meat over when it's in the bag – and you don't even get your hands dirty.

Toasting cumin seeds develops a wonderfully nutty spiciness. Put the seeds in a small dry frying pan and set it over a medium heat. Toast them for a few minutes, shaking the pan occasionally until they start popping, darken in colour and smell fragrant. Grind the seeds in a spice grinder or pulverise them in a mortar with a pestle. When cool, store airtight until required. Some recipes call for no more than a teaspoon of toasted ground cumin seeds – an impossible amount to prepare successfully. It's better to prepare several tablespoons at a time as this will keep well for several weeks.

Pick up

Greek olive oil. As a rule this is not a delicate little thing – it's gutsy. If you can find some, it will add plenty of flavour to these two dishes. Failing Greek oil, use a robust southern Italian oil. Buy a quality red wine vinegar, too, and nice firm kalamata olives.

Essential

Toasted cumin seeds (see opposite) and Greek or Sicilian oregano – they lift this dish into another realm.

Alongside

Serve this at a Sunday barbecue instead of steak. Invite a few friends over, have a bowl of olives and cubes of feta cheese drizzled with garlicky oil and a few squirts of lemon and seasoned with crushed black pepper to nibble on, or some chunks of marinated octopus and roasted salted chickpeas if you want to be really fancy. Fix your favourite aubergine (eggplant) dish – a little Imam Bayildi (garlicky aubergine) perhaps, or barbecued aubergine slices dressed with garlic and lemon – get some decent bread and crisp it in the oven, chill the ouzo and relax. If ouzo's not your thing, go for an easy-drinking dry rosé.

Up front

A cook's dream – marinate the meat the day before and thread it onto skewers on the day. The salad is no big deal, just washing and chopping. Getting the music right on the night is more the worry (no, not Zorba the Greek again!).

X-Factor

Fabulous food – nice lean lamb, full of iron and B vitamins, and all those vegetables, raw and cooked – you'll be able to play up the next day!

1.2kg tender lamb from a prime cut, trimmed and cut into 3cm cubes

2 tablespoons dried Greek or Sicilian oregano

freshly ground black pepper to taste

$1/4$ teaspoon toasted ground cumin seeds (see Titbits below)

3 tablespoons Greek olive oil or southern Italian oil, plus extra for dribbling over the souvlakia before cooking

1 juicy lemon, plus lemon wedges for serving

3 small red onions, peeled and cut into 24 pieces through the root end

2 green peppers (capsicums), halved, cored, deseeded and cut into 24 squares

24 firm sweet cherry tomatoes

sea salt

SERVES 4-6, MAKES ABOUT 24 SKEWERS

Cos Salad

SLICE the red onion, if using, into thin rings and transfer to a bowl of ice-cold water. Leave to soak for 1 hour; this makes the onion crisp and removes strong flavours. Drain and pat dry with absorbent kitchen paper, then put in a large salad bowl with the olives, cucumber, gherkins and cos lettuce.

Sprinkle with the salt and marjoram, then grind on plenty of black pepper. Pour the oil and vinegar over, add the garlic and toss well. Serve immediately, tossing the salad gently at the table.

1 small red onion (optional)
100g (1/2 cup) kalamata olives, drained
1/2 telegraph cucumber (long, tender-skinned cucumber), peeled, halved lengthways, deseeded and cut into chunks
6 gherkins, drained and sliced lengthways
1 cos lettuce, washed, dried and torn into bite-sized pieces
1/2 teaspoon salt
1 teaspoon chopped fresh marjoram
freshly ground black pepper to taste
5 tablespoons extra virgin olive oil (preferably Greek)
1 tablespoon red wine vinegar
1 clove garlic, crushed

SERVES 6

laidback lunches and brunches

Pumpkin and Feta Tart

700g firm-fleshed pumpkin

400g purchased puff pastry, thawed if frozen

1 egg, beaten with a fork

salt to taste

freshly ground black pepper to taste

12 sage leaves

225g (1^1/$_2$ cups) sweet cherry tomatoes, halved

175g firm feta cheese, sliced

1 red onion, sliced

extra virgin olive oil

SERVES 6

CUT the pumpkin into chunks, peel off the skin and remove the seeds. Cut into large cubes and either steam or boil gently until nearly tender; do not overcook. Cool then slice.

Meanwhile, roll the pastry about 44cm long by 26cm wide. Cut off a piece of pastry 20cm long and put the larger piece on a baking sheet lined with baking paper. This larger piece is the base of the pie. Brush around the edges of the pastry with beaten egg. Cut thick strips, about 2cm wide, off the 20cm long piece of pastry, and position these around the edges of the pie base. Chill the pastry until firm.

Brush the strips of pastry around the edges of the pie with beaten egg. Arrange the pumpkin in the centre of the pastry (not on the edges), sprinkle with salt and grind on some black pepper, and scatter the sage leaves over. Next, put in the tomatoes cut side facing up, and cover with the feta and sliced onion.

Drizzle with olive oil. Bake in an oven preheated to 200°C (fanbake) for 20 minutes, or until the pastry is golden brown.

Titbits

This colourful pie is bursting with flavour and it's perfect for a vegetarian main course. If you're having difficulty imagining how the pastry should look, think of it as a picture frame. What you are doing is making a double layer of pastry around the edges of the pie like a frame, so that it will puff and be the same height as the filled centre of the pie once it is baked.

I prefer to steam the pumpkin because it keeps all its flavour and the texture stays firm and dryish – if you turn it into a purée, it's sayonara pumpkin pie.

Pick up

Some grey-skinned pumpkin – I use about a quarter of a large one (it should yield about 500g prepared pumpkin). An oak-aged sauvignon blanc will make a happy partner to this pie.

Essential

Balance – that's what this recipe is all about! Sweet red cherry tomatoes, firm sweet pumpkin that holds its shape, firm feta which loses some of its salt as it browns, and the best puff pastry you can buy.

Alongside

A spinach salad (baby spinach leaves, extra virgin olive oil, lemon juice, crushed garlic, a dab of mustard, salt and black pepper) works a treat with this pie.

Up front

The pastry can be prepared several hours ahead (wrap it tightly and keep it chilled). The pumpkin can be cooked and the feta sliced ahead, but everything else should be done as you assemble the pie. Pastry is always best eaten the day it is made, although leftovers reheat reasonably well.

X-Factor

Ignore the pastry – it's like a sofa for all the other goodies to sit on! It's true it's calorie-laden, but think of the value of onions, tomatoes and extra virgin olive oil – all mentioned elsewhere in the book. Pumpkin is rich in vitamins A and C and has some fibre, and feta is a good, low-fat source of protein.

Niçoise Salad with Flageolet Beans

PUT the dried beans in a bowl and cover with plenty of boiling water. Leave to soak overnight. Drain, rinse and put them in a saucepan. Cover generously with boiling water and bring to the boil. Remove any scum from the surface of the water, then add the bay leaf. Lower the heat, cover with a lid leaving a steam vent, and cook at a gentle boil for 1–2 hours, or until tender (test regularly after the first hour of cooking).

Drain the beans and drape a piece of kitchen paper over the top of them to prevent the surface from drying out as they cool.

Plunge the green beans into a saucepan of gently boiling salted water and cook, uncovered, for several minutes until tender (this salad is not a place for crunchy beans). Drain, rinse with cold water until cool, shake, then dry with absorbent kitchen paper.

Whisk the mustard, garlic, black pepper, oil and vinegar with $1/2$ teaspoon of sea salt.

Shell the eggs carefully and cut them in half.

Choose a large serving bowl, preferably not too deep. Put the cos lettuce in the bowl along with the cucumber, tomatoes and green beans. Add the flageolet beans and scatter the basil over. Pour the dressing on and toss well. Put the eggs, tuna and olives on top, and the anchovies, if using. Toss gently. Serve immediately.

150g dried flageolet beans, or dried beans of your choice
1 fresh bay leaf
250g slim green beans, trimmed
sea salt
1 tablespoon creamy Dijonnaise mustard
2 large cloves garlic, crushed
freshly ground black pepper to taste
1 tablespoon white wine vinegar
3 tablespoons extra virgin olive oil
9 free-range eggs, soft-boiled
1 cos lettuce, washed, dried and torn into bite-sized pieces
1 small telegraph cucumber (long, tender-skinned cucumber), sliced
4 large vine-ripened tomatoes, cut into wedges, cores removed
small handful of baby basil leaves
tuna of your choice
60g ($1/4$ cup) niçoise olives, drained
anchovies in oil, drained (optional)

SERVES 6

Titbits

Ensure the eggs are lightly cooked. I cook medium eggs for 8 minutes (it's important to have them at room temperature before putting them in the saucepan), plunging them into gently boiling water, then lowering the heat so that the water doesn't boil fiercely. Cool the eggs quickly under the running cold tap to stop a grey sulphur ring forming around the yolk. I speed up the process of cooking flageolet beans by pouring boiling water over them to hasten the softening process, but they still need to soak all night in water and take 1½-2 hours to cook. Beans dry out very quickly once drained and can split and become dry.

Pick up

Maille creamy Dijonnaise mustard if possible – it's simply delicious – very creamy and slightly tangy, and it thickens a dressing. It's milder than most mustards so you can use it generously.
Flageolet beans are slim, elongated beans, pale green or cream in colour (there are usually some of each in a bag of beans). They are good in a salad because they hold their shape well. In the mouth they are smooth and slippery until you bite them, then the fluffy, nutty-tasting interior of the beans bursts out. Like all dried beans, they must be cooked until tender (under-cooked beans cause indigestion and flatulence, and in some cases may be toxic). They're fabulous in this salad but, if you can't get them, regular white beans will do.
Use tuna of your choice: several fresh tuna steaks, seared in a hot oiled pan 1 minute each side; 2 x 220g jars Spanish Ortiz tuna, drained; 425g canned tuna in oil, drained.

Essential

Nothing – Niçoise Salad survives the worst insults. What it probably needs more than anything is attitude. It is never passé, it is always easy to put together, and somehow it just emerges time and time again as a crowd pleaser.

Alongside

Good bread, and by that I mean the best loaf you can lay your hands on. Niçoise Salad is satisfying in every way and you can make a meal of it, and every last skerrick should be mopped up with crusty bread and washed down with a good swig of rosé.
You can also serve it as a starter and follow it with small whole fish, panfried in butter until crispy, or barbecued, and served with lemon wedges. All you need is a sunny sky, or moonlight – and, hey!

Up front

Soak and cook the beans ahead. If time is short, use canned beans – just be aware that they are softer than dried, cooked beans, and many are high in sodium (but not so for the organic canned beans I buy). Everything could be chopped ahead of time – but the whole point of a salad like this is to put it together with whatever you have at the time.

X-Factor

This is a major health fest for the mind, body and soul. You can have treble helpings and still feel good about it.

Tomato and Lemon Basil Tarts

2 x 400g packs purchased puff pastry, thawed if frozen

1 egg, lightly beaten with a few pinches of salt

50g (2 cups, loosely packed) lemon basil leaves (use basil if not available)

1kg small vine-ripened tomatoes, thickly sliced

175g jar fiori di cappero (caper flowers), drained

grated zest of 1 lemon

freshly ground black pepper to taste

sea salt

lemon-infused extra virgin olive oil, or the best extra virgin olive oil you can afford

MAKES 12 TARTS

ROLL out each block of pastry to approximately 42cm long by 22cm wide and cut each piece into six rectangles; you don't need a precise size, just think about making each piece big enough to hold a couple of small sliced tomatoes. Transfer the pieces of pastry to oven trays lined with baking paper. Brush the edges of the pastry rectangles with a little beaten egg, then stack the ingredients in the middle of the pastry rectangles in the following order: lemon basil leaves, sliced tomatoes, caper flowers, lemon zest and black pepper. Grind on a little sea salt.

Cook in an oven preheated to 225°C (fanbake) for around 12 minutes, or until the pastry is puffed and a rich golden colour. Drizzle with a little lemon-infused olive oil and serve immediately.

Titbits

Superb! These are not difficult to make, as you can use ready-made pastry, but they taste superb. Serve them as starters (serves 12, one per guest), or make 4–6 main course portions, with salad.

Pick up

The best puff pastry in the land – whichever land you're in!

Lemon basil is the most exquisite herb, imparting the heady, musky, clove-like fragrance of basil with the scent of lemon. It's to die for!

Pinot gris, sauvignon blanc, chardonnay – all will drink comfortably with these tarts.

Essential

Don't bother attempting this with watery or inferior tomatoes. This is the time to pull out the stops and buy exquisite oil, special caper flowers from Italy (sold in jars, in olive oil) and the best commercially made pastry.

Alongside

A little salad of rocket leaves will do nicely.

Up front

You can roll out and cut the pastry hours ahead, but be sure to keep the pastry tightly covered and refrigerated. The rest is just an assembly job.

X-Factor

The whole point of puff pastry is to satiate your soul with the utter delight you get from biting into golden crispy flakes of pastry made with real butter. You should not feel guilt! You do not eat it every day. If you must, focus on the goodness of the tomatoes, capers and basil.

Stirfried Sweet Corn and Red Peppers

REMOVE the husks and silks from the corn cobs, then boil the cobs gently for 12–15 minutes, or until tender. Drain, then cover them with a piece of kitchen paper until cool enough to handle. Cut the kernels off the cobs using a large sharp knife; try to keep the kernels in long strips.

Heat the olive oil in a wok over a medium heat. Add the peppers and stirfry for 3–4 minutes, then add the other ingredients. Toss gently, until everything is piping hot, then tip into a serving bowl.

4 cobs fresh sweet corn

2 tablespoons extra virgin olive oil

2 large red peppers (capsicums), halved, cored, deseeded and cut into thick strips

juice of 1 lime

salt to taste

freshly ground black pepper to taste

2 tablespoons chopped coriander

SERVES 6

Titbits

Read the notes for Summer Sweet Corn and Basil Salad with Avocado (see page 56).

Alongside

Barbecued lamb or pork, or roasted chicken – they are all delicious with this dish. And without a doubt the wine to go with sweet corn is Australian sémillon – there's something about the grassy creaminess that does it.

Up front

The corn could be cooked ahead and, as in the corn salad, you could make it a home for leftover cooked corn cobs (if they're buttered, it won't make any difference). The peppers and coriander can be chopped ahead if need be; keep them covered and chilled.

X-Factor

This has the advantages of sweet corn (carbohydrates, fibre, vitamins A, B, C, potassium), plus a huge dollop of vitamin C from the peppers, and extra from the lime.

Fish Stew with Red and Yellow Peppers and Baby Potatoes

COOK the beans in boiling salted water for 5–10 minutes, drain and refresh; ideally they should be crisp-tender but not crunchy.

Put the extra virgin olive oil, peppers and red onion in a large, deep frying pan. Cook over a medium heat for about 10 minutes, until they are softening and just starting to brown. Put the tomatoes in the pan cut side down and cook for another 3 minutes, squashing them a little with a wooden spoon to release their juices. Season with sea salt and freshly ground black pepper.

Roughly chop the warm potatoes and add them to the pepper stew. Stir well, so they take up some of the flavours. Add the basil leaves and blanched beans. Turn the vegetable stew onto a large serving platter.

Coat half the fish lightly with flour. Meanwhile, have the olive oil heating in a large frying pan and when it is really hot add the fish. Fry quickly until a good golden colour, then turn and cook the second side, caring less about the colour on this side, and making sure that you cook the fish only until it is just approaching being cooked (it will continue cooking as it stands). Transfer the fish to the plate of stewed vegetables, presenting it with the most golden side up. Repeat with the second batch of fish. Toss the vegetables and fish very lightly, then leave to cool to room temperature before serving.

Titbits

The trick with cooking fish in this way is to cook the presentation side first (the side you are going to serve facing up). Choose the most attractive side (the white side free of grey streaks or veins), and let it cook until a good golden colour. Most fish fillets would be overcooked if both sides were cooked until golden, so cook the second side just until the fish is nearly cooked; it'll finish cooking as it stands. This stops the fish from becoming dry, but you still have a good-looking golden side to present, and, if the fish is coated in flour then cooked over a high heat, you'll get some crispy bits, too.

Pick up

White fish fillets that will hold together after cooking – look for a medium-textured fish rather than a soft, flaky fish. Having said that, if you don't mind the look of the fish falling apart (and it can look appetising) go for a soft-textured fish.

Essential

Waxy potatoes. Potatoes fall into three main groups: waxy, all-purpose and starchy. Potatoes with a lot of starch are good for browning. Many have a fluffy interior after cooking which is great for mashing or jacket-baking. Potatoes with a waxy texture hold together after cooking and are good for salads and dishes like this one where you don't want the potatoes to collapse.

Alongside

It's a complete meal on its own, but you could serve a salad of mixed greens as an accompaniment. A New Zealand Marlborough sauvignon blanc with a capsicum character will enhance the peppers in the dish.

Up front

Being a Mediterranean oil-based stew, this is served at room temperature, so it can be completely made up to 2 hours before serving. If you want to make it even earlier than that, and it's okay to make it in advance, keep it covered and refrigerated once it is cool, but bring to room temperature before serving.

X-Factor

Fish is brain food, we all know that, and apparently we don't get enough of it in our diet. Children, in particular, seem reticent to try fish. If they like peppers and basil, this is one way of getting them to tuck in. And don't get anxious about the oil content – just remember that it's dealing to your cholesterol and, as it's rich in vitamin E, it keeps your skin looking young and gorgeous!

200g green beans, trimmed
salt
100ml extra virgin olive oil
2 red and 2 yellow peppers (capsicums), halved, cored, deseeded and cut into chunks
1 large red onion, sliced
8 small vine-ripened tomatoes, halved
sea salt to taste
freshly ground black pepper to taste
750g small new potatoes (choose a salad or waxy type), washed and steamed until tender
handful of basil leaves
1kg skinned and boned white fish fillets, rinsed, patted dry and cut into thirds
45g (1/3 cup) plain flour
100ml olive oil for frying

SERVES 6–8

Summer Corn and Basil Salad with Avocado

4 cobs fresh sweet corn

6 medium vine-ripened tomatoes

1 small red onion, sliced into thin rings

75ml extra virgin olive oil

1½ tablespoons white wine vinegar

20 small basil leaves

¼ teaspoon salt

plenty of freshly ground black pepper

1 ripe but firm avocado

SERVES 8

REMOVE the husks and silks from the corn cobs, then boil the cobs gently for 12–15 minutes, or until tender. Drain, then cover them with a piece of kitchen paper until they are cool enough to handle. Cut the kernels off the cobs using a large sharp knife; try to keep the kernels in long strips.

Cut the tomatoes into wedges and put them in a bowl with the red onion.

In a small bowl blend the olive oil, white wine vinegar, basil, salt and black pepper. Pour this over the tomatoes and onion and toss together. Add the corn and toss gently. Cut the avocado in half, extract the stone, remove the peel and cut the flesh into large cubes or slices. Add to the salad, toss very gently, then serve.

Titbits

There is so much more you can do with sweet corn than slather it in butter (not that there's anything much wrong with eating it like that!). Corn's great in salads and stirfries, and when barbecued or roasted, and it makes a stunning summer soup with cream, lime juice and coriander.

The old wives' tale about not salting the water until the corn is cooked (salt it at the table), because if added during cooking it toughens the kernels, is true.

Pick up

The freshest corn you can because as soon as the sweet corn is cut from the plant, the sugar starts turning to starch, so the sooner you get it in the pot, the sweeter it's going to be. New varieties of corn retain the sugar longer before it converts to starch, but speed is still essential; no amount of care and gentle massaging is going to resurrect withered corn cobs.

Sémillon is fabulous with this.

Essential

The salad's great with barbecued meats, providing colour, juice and crunch.

Up front

The corn can be cooked several hours ahead – at a stretch use leftover corn on the cob (but not if it's been slathered in butter). Assemble everything else just before serving.

X-Factor

Corn is a high-carbohydrate, high-fibre food, with good amounts of vitamins A, B and C. It contains potassium, moderate amounts of protein and hardly any fat, which makes it well worth eating. Add to this mix tomatoes (plenty of vitamin C, some fibre, and vitamins A, and B group) and avocados (all that vitamin E keeps your skin looking younger), and you can start to understand how easy it is to create a bowl full of goodness.

Motorway Chicken

CUT the chicken in half, cutting down each side of the backbone with a pair of scissors or poultry shears, and force it to lie flat (snap the thigh and wing ball and socket joints). Pull off any fat and discard. Rinse the chicken and pat dry with absorbent kitchen paper. Sprinkle the inside of the chicken with a little sea salt, grind on a little black pepper, and add a sprig or two of rosemary or oregano. Transfer it to a roasting tin, turning it skin side up.

Rub the lemon pieces over the chicken skin, squeezing the juice on. Sprinkle the chicken skin with rosemary sprigs or crumbled oregano, and salt, and grind black pepper over, then drizzle the olive oil on top. Put the pieces of lemon in the dish too.

Cook the chicken in an oven preheated to 200°C (regular) for 30 minutes, basting often, then lower the heat to 175°C (fanbake) and cook for about 60 minutes more, basting every 15 minutes. When the chicken is well browned and cooked through, transfer it to a heated serving plate. Cut it into serving pieces using a knife and fork at the table. Garnish with slivers of lemon and fresh rosemary. Squeeze on a little extra lemon juice before serving if liked.

1 free-range, corn-fed organic chicken, about 1.2kg
sea salt
freshly ground black pepper to taste
sprigs of fresh rosemary or Greek or Sicilian dried oregano
$1/2$ lemon, cut in two, and extra lemon wedges for serving
2 tablespoons extra virgin olive oil

SERVES 4

Titbits

I'm not suggesting that you set out looking for road-kill to make this dish – sometimes I get bored with neat little recipe names, and so that I can differentiate one chicken and lemon recipe from another in the filing cabinet in my head, I need a memory tag. Why motorway chicken? Because the chicken is squashed flat.

I'd never seen chicken cooked and presented this way until I went to Greece in the mid-seventies. Mounds of flat, crispy-skinned roasted chickens in food shops tantalised passers-by. All you needed for an outstanding picnic was one of those chickens, a loaf of bread and a bucket of retsina – bliss (apart from the knocking headache from the retsina the next day!).

Rubbing the chicken with lemon and drizzling it with olive oil, then starting the cooking on a high temperature makes the skin pop and sizzle and develop a rich golden colour and gorgeous flavour.

Pick up

Greek or Sicilian oregano. I sometimes use this and the aroma when I rub the flowers and leaves together in the palms of my hands is magic – I could swear that I was back hiking through the hills of Crete crushing wild oregano underfoot. I also love it made with rosemary – that resinous heady perfume it gives off as the spikes turn crispy always induces my hunger and, seemingly, that of anyone else who happens to be in the house, because they start hanging around the kitchen once the chicken starts doing its thing in the oven.

Lots of different wines go with such a simple dish as this – chardonnay, or a lighter red, maybe chianti or rosé, depending on the mood and location.

Essential

A superior chicken that has pecked around in the grass and had a good time on this earth.

Alongside

I like to serve this with a richly flavoured pilaf plumped up with apricots, sultanas, onion and garlic, but you can keep things simple and accompany it with a salad and crusty bread instead. If you want to be naughty and, let's face it, we all want to sometimes, put a few handfuls of roasting potatoes in the dish with the chicken (you won't need to serve rice). They'll absorb all the fat-laden juices coming out of the chicken, turn a rich golden brown and taste sensational.

Up front

The chicken takes no more than 5 minutes to prepare. Then you've got an hour or so to fill in while it cooks. Pour yourself a glass of wine and nibble on a few olives while you listen to the comforting sound of the chicken cooking, drinking in its glorious smells. Cooking shouldn't be all hard work!

X-Factor

If you're a party-pooper, you'll probably put the chicken on a cake rack inside the roasting tin so it is suspended above the gurgling chicken juices and serve it with steamed potatoes – oh well, each to his (or her) own.

Potato Pie

Pastry

575g (about 4 cups) high-grade (strong) flour

a few pinches of salt

300g butter, at room temperature, cut into cubes

150ml cold water

Filling

1kg desiree potatoes, or waxy salad potatoes, peeled and finely sliced

1$^3/_4$ teaspoons salt

1–2 shallots (eschallots), finely chopped

1 tablespoon chopped chervil (optional)

1 tablespoon chopped flat-leafed parsley

2 cloves garlic, finely chopped

freshly ground black pepper to taste

1 egg yolk

250ml cream

SERVES 8 OR MORE

SIFT the flour and a few pinches of salt onto a clean, dry surface. Make a large hollow in the centre, building the flour around the side into a wall. Put the butter in the hollow along with the water, then mix the butter and water with your fingertips. This is really messy, and you need to squelch it together, gradually working in the flour. The liquid is eventually absorbed and a dough forms. Knead thoroughly but lightly, discarding any dry flakes. Form into a ball, wrap and chill for 40 minutes.

Divide the dough in two. Roll one piece into a round 27cm in diameter and put it on a baking sheet lined with baking paper. Cover with waxed paper. Roll the other round 29cm in diameter. Put it on top of the waxed paper, wrap in plastic food wrap and chill until firm.

Put the potatoes in a large bowl and mix in the salt with a large spoon (don't use your hands because the salt will stick to them). Leave for 15 minutes, then pour off any water. Mix in the shallots, chervil if using, parsley, garlic and black pepper.

Put the potatoes in a mound on top of the smaller round of pastry on the baking sheet, keeping them in from the edge. Brush the edge of the dough with beaten egg yolk. Put the second round of dough on top and press the edges together until they stick; trim off any uneven pieces of pastry (use it for making pastry leaves), then carefully curl the sealed edges into the pie, so they are enclosed in the roll (the pie must be well sealed). Use the back edge of the blade of a thin bladed knife to mark the edge of the pastry into a scallop pattern.

Make a small steam hole in the centre of the pastry, just big enough to fit the spout of a small funnel. Lightly score the surface of the pastry with the tip of a sharp knife. If liked, roll any scraps of pastry and cut into pastry leaves. Position them around the steam hole, sticking them on with egg yolk. Mix a few drops of water into the egg yolk and brush it over the pie.

Bake in an oven preheated to 200°C (regular) for 1$^1/_4$ hours, lowering the heat to 170°C once the pastry is nicely browned. Remove the pie from the oven, put the funnel in the steam hole and slowly pour in the cream a few tablespoons at a time; it will take several minutes to absorb it. Leave the pie until cool. Serve at room temperature.

Titbits

This is a magnificent pie based on a recipe by Roger Vergé. It's grand enough for the grandest picnic, but it's also stunning as part of a buffet. Allow time to rest the dough before rolling it out, to minimise shrinkage. If you inadvertently forget the dough and it hardens, leave it to soften at room temperature before rolling it.

Pick up

UK readers should use a mixture of 150ml double cream and 100ml single cream. Make sure the potatoes are the waxy type – starchy potatoes will turn to a soft fluff. You could match richness with richness and serve this with a big creamy chardonnay but, for me,

the thrill of a high-acid sauvignon blanc cutting through the creaminess is much more appealing.

Alongside

A salad of interesting crisp green leaves. But it is also superb if served warmish with a huge mound of steaming asparagus and a slice or two of ham off the bone.

Up front

There's no pretending that this pie is quick to prepare – but you can get things well organised ahead of time. The pastry can be prepared up to a day ahead; roll it, wrap it tightly and chill until required. If absolutely

necessary, the pie can be cooked the day before required; when it is completely cool, wrap it and refrigerate. Bring it to room temperature before serving, or warm it briefly in a moderate oven.

X-Factor

Don't get upset about the amount of salt, cream and butter – sometimes food needs all these things to make it taste delicious. Think instead of the goodness in potatoes, shallots, garlic and herbs – and all the goodies in the salad that you MUST serve with it.

South Pacific Fish Cakes with Coconut and Lime

900g skinned and boned white fish fillets, preferably a type which flakes easily, rinsed and patted dry

olive oil

60ml (¼ cup) canned coconut cream

35g (½ cup) desiccated coconut

4 tablespoons fresh breadcrumbs, plus a little more if necessary

½ teaspoon salt

1 teaspoon raw sugar

2 tablespoons finely chopped coriander

2 tablespoons plain flour

1 egg

Coconut Dressing

4 tiny dried 'bird's eye' chillies, crushed

120ml thick canned coconut cream

4 kaffir lime leaves

Lime Dressing

1 fresh, juicy lime

4 tiny dried 'bird's eye' chillies, crushed

4 tablespoons extra virgin olive oil

4 kaffir lime leaves

MAKES ABOUT 16 SMALL CAKES (SERVE 2 FOR A STARTER, OR 4 FOR A MAIN COURSE WITH OTHER DISHES)

SMEAR the fish fillets on both sides with olive oil. Cook on a barbecue hotplate over a medium heat, turning once carefully with a fish slice, until nearly cooked through. Cool briefly, then flake with a fork and place in a bowl. Beat in the rest of the ingredients. Shape into fish cakes and refrigerate until ready to cook.

Heat a little olive oil in a large frying pan (or use a wok attachment on a barbecue). Alternatively, cook the fish cakes on a greased barbecue hotplate. Cook the fish cakes until golden on both sides (treat them carefully because they are soft and delicate), drain briefly, then serve hot with either the coconut or lime dressing. Alternatively, serve with a ready-made peanut sauce.

To make the coconut dressing, put all the ingredients in a small pan and simmer gently until reduced by about half. Set aside until ready to use.

To make the lime dressing, remove the rind from the lime using a small serrated knife, then cut in between the membrane to release the small pieces of lime fillet. Cut these into small pieces and add to the other ingredients in a bowl, adding any lime juice.

Titbits

If you're a fisherperson (I should say, a lucky fisherperson), this is a great way to use up excess freshly caught fish. Cook the fish, eat what you want for the first meal, then refrigerate the leftovers and turn them into these fish cakes the next day. Of course, you can make them with fish from the local fish shop, and cook the fillets indoors in a frying pan.

The sauces give the fish cakes a pungent, spicy hit.

Pick up

Coconut cream, not coconut milk, for the sauce, because it is rich and thick. The cream tends to settle on the top of a can of coconut cream. Let the can stand, open it carefully, and spoon off the thick cream for the sauce, then take the thinner mixture for the fish cakes. Use any leftover coconut liquid in a rice dish of your choice. If coconut cream is not available, use a double quantity of coconut milk and reduce it by half in a saucepan over a medium heat until it is thick. If you can't find kaffir lime leaves, don't use dried kaffir leaves. Substitute fresh, unblemished lemon tree leaves, washed, rolled up and sliced into shreds – they're nearly as good.

Essential

Fresh limes.

Alongside

Ban sausages and steaks and make these fishcakes part of an Asian-inspired outdoor summer barbecue feast. Assemble a mountain of prawns, crabs and crays, and drizzle them with hot Asian sauces. Maybe throw together a salad of cooling cucumber and mint, and add some green mango, shredded ginger, lime and crushed roasted peanuts to go with it.

If you're going for wine, pick up a fruity riesling (a big chardonnay will be too rich, a sauvignon blanc too acid).

Up front

Make and shape the fishcakes and keep them refrigerated until ready to cook them.

X-Factor

The jury is still out about coconut – it may be high in saturated fat – but it may differ from the harmful type found in animal and dairy fats. Keep your fingers crossed! Fish generally is a great source of low-fat protein.

Berry Compote with Cinnamon Toasts

300g (2 cups) strawberries, sliced

300g (2 cups) cherries, pitted

300g (2 cups) raspberries

150g (1 cup) blackberries

150g (1 cup) blueberries

grated zest and juice of 1 lemon

3 tablespoons icing sugar, or to taste

1 loaf sweet raisin or brioche bread, thickly
    sliced, or 3 chocolate bread rolls, sliced

unsalted butter, softened

2 tablespoons caster sugar mixed with
    1 teaspoon ground cinnamon

crème fraîche, yoghurt or cream for
    serving

SERVES 6

PUT all the fruit in a large bowl with the lemon zest and juice and add icing sugar to taste. Chill.

At serving time, toast the bread under the grill on one side. Spread the untoasted side with butter, then sprinkle thickly with cinnamon sugar. Grill slowly, not too close to the source of heat, until the toasts are golden brown. Cut into fingers and serve hot with chilled berries and crème fraîche.

Titbits

You can, if need be, make this using frozen raspberries, blackberries and blueberries. If there are no fresh cherries, leave them out. I don't think frozen strawberries are worth considering because they turn too slushy when thawed.

Pick up

A brioche loaf if possible. I have made these toasts successfully with all the breads mentioned, but probably my favourite is a brioche – it is made with a lot of butter, so be sparing with any butter you spread on.

Up front

Raspberries, blackberries and blueberries all keep well in the lemon juice and sugar marinade for a day or two, but strawberries and cherries do not. If you want to make this ahead, add the strawberries and cherries at the last minute (you could stone the cherries ahead; put them in a covered container and keep them refrigerated).

X-Factor

The berries are full of goodies such as the antioxidants vitamins C and E, fibre and anthocyanins (the pigments that give the berries their colour). If you wanted to bump up the vitamin C content, throw in a handful of blackcurrants, and if you are prone to cystitis, add some cranberries.

Potato Tortilla with Chorizo

1 soft chorizo sausage (about 100g), sliced

650g (4 medium) new to mid-season
    potatoes

190ml ($^3/_4$ cup) olive oil

1 small onion, sliced

4 free-range eggs

$^1/_2$ teaspoon salt

SERVES 6-10 AS A TAPA

HEAT a smallish oiled frying pan over a high heat. When the pan is hot, put in the chorizo and cook for about 30 seconds, until the edges just start to curl and colour. Turn each slice over and repeat. Turn off the heat and tilt the pan to allow any fat to run off. Scoop out the chorizo with a slotted spoon and drain briefly on absorbent kitchen paper. This operation should be carried out swiftly or the chorizo can burn.

Peel the potatoes and cut into slices 3mm thick. Pat dry with a clean cloth or absorbent kitchen paper.

Use a 20cm non-stick frying pan. Heat the olive oil in the pan over a medium heat. Slip in the potato slices carefully, then turn the heat to low. Cover with a lid or a large dinner plate and cook for 5 minutes. Turn the potatoes carefully, then put the onion on top and continue cooking for 10 minutes, turning once or twice, or until the potatoes are tender but not browned. Tip the potatoes and onion into a strainer set over a bowl and drain briefly.

Put the eggs and salt in a large bowl and beat until the eggs are broken up. Add the drained potatoes and onion and chorizo, and mix in; leave for 10 minutes or longer – up to 2 hours.

Wipe out the pan with absorbent kitchen paper and add 2 tablespoons of the drained oil (the rest can be reused; strain it into a container, leaving the starch behind). Set the pan over a high heat, swirl the oil around the sides of the pan and, once the oil is hot, tip in the egg mixture and immediately turn the heat to low. Cook gently until a light golden brown on the bottom. Place a large plate over the pan and invert the tortilla onto it. Quickly slide the tortilla back into the pan (if the pan is dry, add a little oil first) and cook the second side gently until a light golden colour.

Alternatively, slide the tortilla onto a large plate, cover with a second plate, invert, and slide back into the pan uncooked side down.

Slide the cooked tortilla onto a serving plate. Cool, then serve at room temperature, cut into wedges or cubes.

Titbits

Potato tortilla is served in tapas bars throughout Spain. Adding chorizo sausage gives a spicy sweet flavour. The potatoes and onion need to be cooked slowly in a generous amount of oil, which gives the tortilla a meltingly tender quality, and prevents it from becoming dry and eggy (but 80% of the oil is strained off and can be reused). It's essential that the oil is hot when the potato and egg mixture goes back into the pan so that the egg puffs up around the sides (this prevents it sticking to the pan, too). Lower the heat immediately, so the tortilla cooks gently and the inside remains creamy.

Pick up

Potatoes that will keep their shape, not collapse into fluff. The best are waxy potatoes about halfway through their season, when they're just starting to develop a little starch.

Essential

Good chorizo sausage that has a firmish texture and enough bite to wake your taste buds up. If you can't find anything to match this description, or if you're a vegetarian, omit the sausage.

Alongside

It's delightful with a glass of chilled Tio Pepe, or a glass of red Navarra from Spain. It easily fits in with other tapas dishes to form a feast, or it can be served as a luncheon dish with a salad of sliced tomatoes and sliced oranges with a good squirt of lemon juice, fresh mint and pungent extra virgin olive oil.

Up front

It's one of those kind-to-the-cook dishes that must be made in advance. I think it is at its stunning best while still warm from the pan.

X-Factor

Yes, yes, yes! Think of all the vitamin C, potassium and fibre in potatoes, and the goodness of onion, all mixed with that poor underrated storehouse of goodies – the egg!

Slow-roasted Tomatoes

HALVE the tomatoes and put them in a shallow ovenproof tray (I use a non-stick Swiss roll tin) cut side up. Distribute a little sea salt, black pepper and sugar over the cut surfaces and drizzle with a little oil. Bake in an oven preheated to 140°C (regular) for about 1 hour, or until the tomatoes have collapsed and the juices are syrupy.

500g small plum tomatoes or vine-ripened tomatoes
sea salt
freshly ground black pepper to taste
caster sugar
extra virgin olive oil

Titbits

Cooking tomatoes slowly in the oven with a little seasoning and olive oil has an extraordinary effect upon them. Some of their water content evaporates, which is not a bad thing, and their flesh becomes meltingly tender. But it's what happens to the taste that turns them into showstoppers. The very essence of the tomatoes' sweetness and fruitiness is intensified and the juices turn syrupy and develop hints of caramel during the slow baking. They're simply gorgeous!

Uses

With avocado on top of grilled/barbecued/panfried fish:

Rinse and pat dry firm fish fillets. Dust with flour. Fry quickly in hot olive oil. Alternatively, oil the fillets and grill or barbecue them. Put the fish fillets on a serving platter. Top with chunks of avocado and slow-roasted tomatoes. Whip the top off a bottle of sauvignon blanc to go with it.

On pasta with caper berries:

Cook Italian egg pasta (dried rich yellow pasta) in boiling salted water until al dente. Drain. Toss slow-roasted tomatoes, capers or caper berries, basil leaves and slivers of parmigiano reggiano through the pasta. Open a cheeky and affordable bottle of chianti and dig in!

For the best BLT:

Buy very fresh, long-sliced wholegrain bread. Smear with salad cream or mayonnaise. Make a sandwich with iceberg lettuce, crispy bacon, chunks of avocado and slow-roasted tomatoes. Cut sandwiches in half and devour with chilled lager.

On toasted panini topped with hummus, crisp bacon and coriander:

I like to make my own hummus because so many taste of rank garlic. You simply squish (or process) very tender chick peas (they must be cooked until they are squishable) with tahini, lemon juice, fresh crushed garlic and salt. Toast a panini, slather with hummus and top with slow-roasted tomatoes, crispy bacon and a generous covering of chopped coriander. A chilled sémillon with this combo will see you right.

With panfried chicken breasts and orzo:

Panfry chicken breasts in the normal way (skinned, floured, slipped into sizzling butter, on medium heat) and add chopped tarragon, rosemary or sage leaves and transfer to a platter. Top with slow-roasted tomatoes and serve with a mountain of orzo tossed with lemon oil and sea salt. This is chardonnay country.

On bruschetta with tapenade and baby salad leaves:

Toast sliced ciabatta over barbecue flames (or in the toaster if that's easier), rub with a cut clove of garlic and arrange on plates. Spread generously with black olive tapenade, top with baby leaves and slow-roasted tomatoes. Time to crack open a nippy chianti.

Up front

The tomatoes will keep for up to a week in a covered container in the refrigerator, so they're there when you need them.

X-Factor

There's a big whack of the antioxidant lycopene in tomatoes, so all of these dishes have a healthy base.

Pigs in Blankets

12 slim sausages

olive oil

soft flour tortillas, or purchased ready-
    rolled puff pastry, thawed if frozen

1 egg, lightly beaten

Flame-roasted Tomato and Chilli Salsa
    (see page 91)

SERVES 6

COOK the sausages in a hot pan with a little oil, or on a barbecue. Don't overcook them if making pigs in pastry blankets because they will continue cooking in the oven.

To make pigs in pastry blankets, cut a sheet of rolled pastry into long strips 2.5cm wide. Brush the strips of pastry with beaten egg, then wrap around the lightly cooked, drained sausages. Put the pigs in blankets on a tray lined with baking paper, brush with more egg and bake in an oven preheated to 200°C (fanbake) for 20–25 minutes or until a good golden colour.

If using soft flour tortillas, wrap them in kitchen paper then warm them in a microwave, or wrap them in tin foil and warm them in an oven preheated to 180°C (regular). Wrap half a tortilla around each sausage (snip the tortillas with scissors).

Serve hot with the Flame-Roasted Tomato and Chilli Salsa (see page 91).

Titbits

Kids will love the name of what is simply sausages wrapped in pastry or tortillas, and will enjoy helping. With a bit of luck you can pass the job over to them and get breakfast cooked for you!

Pick up

Decent sausages – not ones full of cheap fillers.

Essential

The Flame-Roasted Salsa – it turns the pigs in blankets into adult fare.

Alongside

You could go the whole hog (ha ha!) and serve this with Slow-roasted Tomatoes (see page 65), or oven-baked/grilled/barbecued tomatoes, crisp and crunchy rashers of bacon, and creamed sweet corn, for a brunch to remember.

Up front

It's just as easy to cook the sausages and wrap them in one go.

X-Factor

Who are you kidding? Pastry and sausages, served with a fry-up of bacon? Go for a run around the block later in the day and eat salad the next night for dinner.

Roasted Chicken with Rosemary Potatoes and Barbecued Vegetables

RINSE the chicken inside and out, removing any lumps of fat. Drain, then pat dry with absorbent kitchen paper. Put a knob of butter inside the chicken, along with a sprig of tarragon, a little salt and black pepper and the garlic. Tie the chicken legs together with string, hooking the string around the parson's nose to keep the cavity closed, then put the chicken in a smallish roasting tin – choose one in which it fits snugly. Pour in the chicken stock. Melt 25g butter and brush over the chicken. Squeeze a little lemon juice on and sprinkle with salt. Put the chicken in an oven preheated to 180°C (regular) and cook for about 1¹/₂ hours, basting often (turn the chicken over after 20 minutes, cook for a further 20 minutes, then turn breast uppermost again for the rest of the cooking).

The chicken should be kept moist during cooking; add more stock if it dries up. Halfway through cooking, or when you turn the chicken breast up again, strew it generously with plenty of tarragon sprigs, which will turn deliciously crisp.

Remove the chicken from the oven when it is cooked through to the bone and let it rest at room temperature for 1¹/₂-2 hours, covered with a ventilated cover, keeping the tarragon on a separate plate to keep it crisp. Serve with Rosemary Potatoes and Barbecued Vegetables (see page 69).

Chicken

1 free-range, corn-fed organic chicken, about 1.3kg
butter
generous handful of fresh tarragon
salt
freshly ground black pepper to taste
1 clove garlic, lightly crushed
250ml (1 cup) chicken stock (more if needed)
1¹/₂ lemons

SERVES 6

Titbits

Don't throw your arms up in horror at the idea of leaving the chicken at room temperature for 1¹/₂ hours after cooking. This allows the chicken to reabsorb all its juices, which makes the flesh beautifully succulent. The chicken will still be warm and will fall off the bones. Chicken caught at this perfect moment, before it cools and the flesh sets, is a joy to eat.

Pick up

Maille Dijonnaise mustard (a very creamy, slightly tangy mustard) if you can.

Essential

Good ingredients – loads of basil and French tarragon, a good-tasting chicken, premium extra virgin olive oil, good wine vinegar and good mustard. Anything else makes a pale imitation of the real thing.

Alongside

This is pretty well a complete meal – chicken, potatoes and vegetables – but you could serve it as part of a buffet. And chardonnay is the wine to serve with it.

Up front

The chicken can be prepared ready for roasting several hours ahead, but is best eaten the day it is roasted, while the meat is succulent and falls off the bones. The potatoes can be peeled an hour before required; wrap them in a damp tea towel. Don't chop the rosemary and garlic until the potatoes are nearly ready, although the garlic can be peeled ahead. The barbecued vegetables can be prepared 3–4 hours ahead; keep them covered at room temperature. Make the dressing at serving time.

X-Factor

It's so boring not eating chicken skin, especially when it's all golden and crisp and dripping flavoursome juices. But I have it on good authority that eating chicken skin with the meat increases the fat content three-fold! It's too sad. My motto is, only eat it when it is absolutely irresistible, never when it is limp and past its best (applies to anything, really). But you should generally feel quite good about eating this dish. I've used olive oil where I can instead of butter, there's garlic for goodness, and lots of herbs and vegetables.

Rosemary Potatoes and Barbecued Vegetables

PREPARE the potatoes. Turn the potato cubes onto a clean teatowel or absorbent kitchen paper and pat dry. Tip them into a shallow oven dish and pour the oil over. Season with salt and black pepper, then toss the potatoes so that they are all covered in oil. Dot the dish with butter. Bake the potatoes in an oven preheated to 200°C (fanbake) for 1 hour or until crisp and golden. Remove the dish from the oven, add the chopped rosemary and garlic, stir well and return the potatoes to the oven for 5 more minutes.

When the potatoes are in the oven, prepare the other vegetables. Put them in a large bowl, drizzle with a little extra virgin olive oil and season with salt and black pepper. Cook them on a hot barbecue plate until browned, keeping them crisp-tender (alternatively, put them in a shallow roasting tin and roast in a hot oven for around 40 minutes).

Put all the dressing ingredients, except the basil, in a small bowl and mix together. To finish off, put the barbecued vegetables on a large platter and top with the potatoes and all their garlicky bits. Break the chicken into rough joints or chunks with a cleaver and arrange on top of the vegetables, pouring any juices over. Remix the dressing, adding the basil and spoon it over the chicken. Garnish with lemon wedges, arrange the crispy tarragon on top and serve immediately.

Rosemary Potatoes

1.5kg roasting potatoes, peeled and cubed
50ml olive oil
³/₄ teaspoon salt
freshly ground black pepper to taste
a little butter
2 tablespoons rosemary spikes
4 large cloves garlic, very finely chopped

Barbecued Vegetables

2 yellow peppers (capsicums), halved, cored, deseeded and cut into chunks
3 red onions, peeled and cut into chunks through the root end
4 courgettes (zucchini) – opt for 2 yellow and 2 green if available – trimmed and cut in half lengthways and scored lightly with the point of a sharp knife
extra virgin olive oil
salt to taste
freshly ground black pepper to taste

Dressing

2 tablespoons creamy Dijonnaise mustard
freshly ground black pepper to taste
2 tablespoons white wine vinegar
6 tablespoons extra virgin olive oil
1¹/₂ teaspoons salt
handful of fresh basil leaves

SERVES 6

Roasted Chicken with Rosemary Potatoes and Barbecued Vegetables

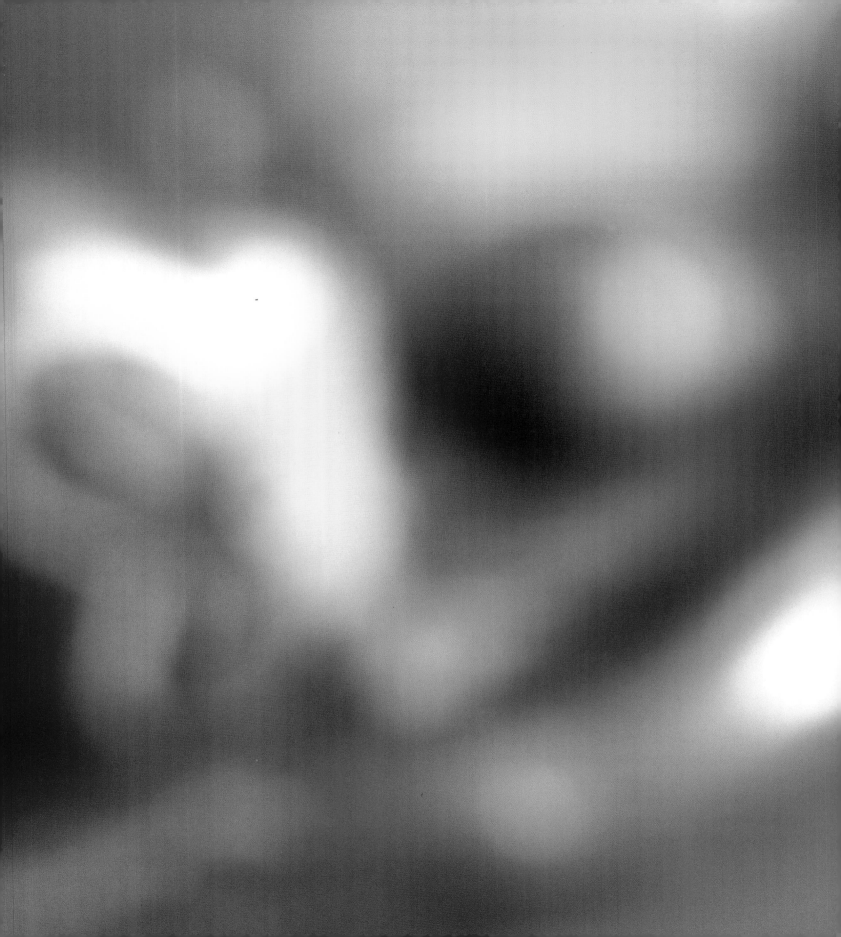

indian summer

Prawn and Feta Skewers with Snow Pea and Cucumber Salad

24 large green king prawns (if frozen, thaw
   slowly in the refrigerator)
400g feta cheese, cut into cubes
small bamboo skewers about 15cm long
75ml (1/3 cup) lemon-infused extra virgin
   olive oil
freshly ground black pepper to taste

200g snow peas, topped and tailed
1 small telegraph cucumber (long, tender-
   skinned cucumber), cut into chunks
30g (1 cup) coriander leaves
225g (1 1/2 cups) sweet cherry tomatoes
sea salt

SERVES 4–6

PREPARE the prawns first. Twist off the heads, then peel off the shells, leaving the small piece of shell on the tail intact. Slit down the back of each prawn with a sharp knife and gently extract the black or orangey-red vein running lengthways. Rinse and pat dry with absorbent kitchen paper.

Cut the feta into cubes and skewer 2 prawns and 1–2 pieces of feta on each skewer. The cheese is less likely to split if you screw the skewers through the cheese rather than push it in. (If this operation proves difficult – the feta splits, the skewers don't perform – simply put the prawns and feta cubes on an oiled baking sheet and cook as described.)

Put the skewers on an oiled baking sheet and drizzle generously with lemon-infused extra virgin olive oil. Grind on some pepper. Cook under a hot grill until the prawns are pink and the feta has browned. Carefully turn the skewers over and grill the second side. Have the salad ready and put the prawn skewers on top. Drizzle with a little more lemon oil and serve immediately.

To make the salad, blanch the snow peas quickly in a saucepan of boiling water (leave them in the water for about 30 seconds). Drain, rinse with plenty of cold water, then pat dry with absorbent kitchen paper. Put the cucumber, coriander leaves, cherry tomatoes and snow peas on a large platter, toss them gently and grind on a little black pepper and add a few pinches of sea salt – nothing else.

Titbits

It probably seems strange not to toss the salad with a dressing, but it doesn't need it. It's wonderfully juicy and crisp and the coriander provides plenty of flavour. A little bit of salt and black pepper lifts it all, and then there are the delicious flavours of the lemon oil, prawns and feta.

Pick up

A dryish firm feta, not a squidgy soft type.

Essential

Lemon-infused olive oil – it makes the dish (if you have to use a substitute, go for the best extra virgin olive oil you have and add the finely grated zest of a lemon).

Alongside

You could follow this with more fish. Although not traditional, you could try it with a seafood and tomato risotto (traditionally, a risotto would be served as a first course). An oak-aged sauvignon blanc will work wonders with these flavours.

Up front

The prawns can be prepared up to 24 hours in advance, then covered and refrigerated. You can start on the vegetables about 1 hour before finishing off the dish.

X-Factor

Prawns contain vitamin B12, niacin, calcium, phosphorous, iodine, selenium – goodies which makes the cost of them a little easier to justify.

Turkey Breast in Verjuice with Green Grapes and Almonds

PAT the turkey breasts dry with absorbent kitchen paper. Set a large ovenproof casserole that will fit the turkey breasts comfortably without overcrowding over a medium heat and, when hottish, drop in 1 tablespoon of olive oil and a knob of butter. While the butter is sizzling, put in the turkey breasts (with what was the skin side facing down) and brown well on both sides. Season with a little salt and black pepper, add the garlic and 1 tablespoon of the chopped tarragon. Cook for 1 minute, until the garlic is browning, then spoon some of the garlicky mixture on top of the turkey breasts.

Pour in the verjuice and immediately cover with a lid. Transfer to an oven preheated to 180°C (fanbake) and cook for 15–20 minutes, or until the meat is just cooked through but is still very juicy (remember it will continue to cook as it stands).

While the turkey is cooking, skin the grapes. This sounds fiddly, but it doesn't take a minute and it ensures you don't end up with tough or tannic skins spoiling the sauce. Put the prepared grapes in a cup with the lemon juice.

When the turkey breasts are ready, remove the dish from the oven and leave it covered with the lid for 5 minutes.

Transfer the turkey breasts to a board and attend to the juices. Scoop off any fat, then bubble up the juices and add the cream. Reduce for a few minutes until thickish, add the grapes and lemon juice, the almonds and the rest of the tarragon leaves. Season lightly. Slice the turkey breasts across the grain and arrange on a heated plate. Spoon the sauce over them and serve immediately.

2 single turkey breasts, skinned, weighing about 500g each
1 tablespoon olive oil
small knob of butter
salt
freshly ground black pepper to taste
2 cloves garlic, finely chopped
2 tablespoons chopped fresh tarragon, plus some whole leaves
60ml (1/4 cup) verjuice, or use dry white wine or light chicken stock
170g (1 cup) seedless green grapes, peeled
juice of 1 lemon
60ml (1/4 cup) cream
1/2 cup flaked almonds, lightly toasted

SERVES 6

Titbits

Turkey breast meat is mild to taste, and is tender and succulent to eat. It absorbs other flavours well – a bit like chicken, it's what you put with it that makes the dish exceptional. You can make it a special occasion dish, Christmas for instance.

I cook the turkey breasts in a shallow casserole rather than a high-sided one. The vessel you use and the thermostat of your oven may well produce a different result – 20 minutes' cooking time is a guide.

I know, I know, who wants to peel grapes? It's such a cliché, but in this dish it really makes a difference – unless you happen to have fabulous soft-skinned non-tannic grapes. If the grapes have seeds, halve them and pick or flick out the seeds. The prepared grapes will hold about an hour in the lemon juice.

Pick up

Verjuice – unfermented grape juice. It is mildly acidic and pleasantly refreshing without the lingering acidity of say, lemon. It doesn't quite have lemon's freshness, but

that means it can blend into the background and add a flavour note without being overbearing. Once opened, keep it refrigerated – it should last for ages.

Alongside

If you're serving this in place of the usual stuffed turkey on Christmas day, I would sizzle some smallish cubes of kumara (sweet potato) in butter until crisp to go with it. (Cut the kumara into cubes, put in a shallow ovenproof dish, drizzle with a little oil and roast on high until crunchy. If liked, top with a little chopped crisp bacon.) If you're in the southern hemisphere, serve the roasted kumara and turkey with colourful vegetables such as asparagus, mixed green and butter beans, sweet cherry tomatoes, snow peas or sugar snaps. In cooler climes, go for a similar mélange but using baby carrots and turnips, and tight-budded Brussels sprouts, mixed with panfried shallots (eschallots) and sweet cherry tomatoes for colour.

This dish is delicious with a creamy, yeasty champagne or bubbly – my pick is Cloudy

Bay's very elegant vintage méthode Pelorus, named after the dolphin in the Marlborough Sounds, New Zealand.

Up front

You can toast the almonds 2 hours ahead; once cool, keep airtight. The grapes can be done an hour ahead. The garlic peeled (not chopped) 24 hours ahead (cover and refrigerate). Everything else is put together as you cook the dish.

X-Factor

Turkey breast meat is low in fat and high in protein – everything you want from a meat – and it contains selenium and most of the B group vitamins.

South Seas Fish in Coconut Cream Sauce

1.25kg golden kumara (sweet potato), peeled and cubed

salt

1 small, perfectly ripe pineapple

100g butter

1 tablespoon coriander seeds, crushed (use a spice grinder or mortar and pestle)

grated zest of 1 lemon

freshly ground black pepper to taste

1kg smallish skinned and boned white fish fillets, rinsed, patted dry and cut into thirds

4–6 large shallots (eschallots), thinly sliced (about 1 cup sliced shallots)

2 fresh hot red chillies, halved, deseeded and finely chopped

1 tablespoon olive oil

2 red peppers (capsicums), halved, cored, deseeded and cut into chunks

400ml coconut cream

handful of fresh mint leaves

6 fresh lemon leaves, sliced very finely

SERVES 6 GENEROUSLY

COOK the kumara in gently boiling salted water until nearly tender; don't overcook. Drain. Prepare the pineapple by peeling it, removing the core and cutting the flesh into slices (this is easily done with a nifty gadget called a pineapple corer which removes the skin and core while cutting the flesh into a continuous ring).

Melt all but 2 tablespoons of the butter and add the coriander seeds, lemon zest and pepper. Pass the fish fillets through the melted butter and lay them on a tray. Keep chilled.

Put a smallish frying pan over a low to medium heat and add the rest of the butter. While the butter is sizzling, add the shallots. Cook gently until golden, about 30 minutes (don't hurry this or the shallots will burn), then add the chopped chillies. Cook for 2–3 minutes more.

When ready to put the meal together, bring the fish to room temperature. Cook the pieces of fish in batches in a hot oiled non-stick pan (or on a barbecue plate) until golden and just cooked through. Transfer them to a plate as they are done.

Lastly, cook the peppers. Heat the olive oil in a large frying pan or wok over a medium-high heat and when the oil is hot add the peppers. Stirfry for about 5 minutes, until just starting to wilt, then add the kumara, pineapple and coconut cream. Season with salt and cook, stirring, until the coconut cream is bubbling and has reduced a little. Stir the mint through, then turn the vegetables onto a large platter. Top with the fish fillets, garnish with finely sliced lemon leaves and serve immediately.

Titbits

Using the leaves of lemon trees is quite safe, providing the tree hasn't been sprayed. The leaves should be young and supple, and sliced exceedingly finely. Substitute kaffir lime leaves if not available.

Pick up

Coconut cream (not milk) – I buy Samoan coconut cream. If you use thin coconut milk, you will need to reduce the sauce much longer – it may be a good idea to remove the vegetables to a side bowl while you do this to avoid them becoming mushy. Choose a firm kumara, one that will hold its shape after cooking. The fish needs to be a firm-fleshed variety.

Alongside

Fragrant steamed Thai or basmati rice and other Pacific-style dishes, or seafood dishes will work well. Try to balance the richness of the coconut by serving at least some of the dishes with fresh flavours of lemon, lime, chilli and mint. And go for a crisp New Zealand sauvignon blanc and let the biting-crisp acids cut a swathe through the richness of the dish.

Up front

The fish can be prepared several hours before cooking; keep it covered and refrigerated. The shallots can be cooked 1 hour ahead. The pineapple can be prepared several hours ahead; keep it covered and refrigerated. The kumara can be cooked 2–3 hours ahead; keep at room temperature. The peppers can be cut into chunks and kept refrigerated until required.

X-Factor

Coconut is high in saturated fat, but continuing studies may reveal that it works differently in the body to saturated animal fat. Pineapple contains some antioxidants and is very good for digestion. Peppers, chillies and shallots, along with fish, make this an exceptionally nutritious dish. Choose orange-skinned, orange-fleshed kumara over purple skinned, white-fleshed kumara because they contain more beta-carotene. Both have dollops of the antioxidants vitamins C and E.

Feta in Piquillo Peppers with Squished Black Olive Dressing

200g firm feta cheese, sliced into long thin
   pieces, enough so that there is one for
   each pepper
2 x 250g jars piquillo peppers (make sure
   you buy whole peppers, not sliced ones),
   drained (reserve the juices)
sprigs of fresh rosemary
1 clove garlic, crushed
1½ tablespoons lemon juice
2 soft black olives, stoned and mashed
   to a paste
1 tablespoon Spanish extra virgin olive oil

SERVES 6 AS A TAPA

PUT a chunk of feta in each pepper and arrange the peppers on a large platter. Chop some rosemary spikes very finely and transfer to a small bowl (you'll need half a teaspoon of chopped rosemary). Add the garlic, lemon juice, mashed olives and olive oil. Mix well, adding the pepper juices. Spoon the dressing over the peppers, garnish with a few sprigs of rosemary and serve.

Titbits

Simple, gutsy-flavoured tapas which takes no more than 10 minutes to put together. To make them more substantial, serve the peppers on top of hunks of good bread – you'll need plates and cutlery. To make them suitable for vegetarians, opt for a cheese made with something other than rennet, and choose whatever type of feta you prefer – cow's, goat's, or ewe's.

Essential

Spanish piquillo peppers (see page 22). If you can't get them, make something else.

Alongside

Fix a variety of other tapas and invite over a gaggle of girls and guys and feast up large. This will work well with pinot noir – it'll like the peppers and earthy tones of the olives – and go exceptionally well with cabernet sauvignon because the sweet fruit will hitch up with the peppers and the savouriness of rosemary and olives. Or make a light, refreshing version of sangria with red or rosé wine, soda, ice, smashed lemon grass, strawberries and lemon leaves.

Up front

Most of the components of this dish can be prepared in advance (crush the olives, peel the garlic, drain the peppers, slice the feta), but mix everything together and pour it over the peppers just before serving. Another point – rosemary darkens soon after chopping, so if you want nice green flecks of rosemary, chop it just before mixing the dressing and serving the peppers.

X-Factor

Red peppers are dripping with vitamins C and A – you can feel the goodness seep into your bones like sunshine as you eat into them.

Orange and Tuna Salad

250g (about 4) small, waxy salad potatoes
salt
220g bottled Spanish white tuna, drained
   and broken apart into chunks
3 juicy oranges
3 tablespoons Spanish extra virgin olive oil
1 tablespoon red wine vinegar
2 large cloves garlic, finely chopped
2 tablespoons flat-leafed parsley
1/2 teaspoon smoked hot Spanish paprika
freshly ground black pepper to taste
20 green, black or pimento-stuffed Spanish
   olives

SERVES 6 AS A TAPA

COOK the potatoes gently in boiling salted water until just tender. Cool, peel then slice. Put the sliced potatoes in a shallow dish. Flake the drained tuna with a fork and put on top of the potatoes.

Peel 2 oranges, removing all the white pith, then cut into segments, leaving the pithy part behind (squeeze out any juice in the membrane and reserve). Put the orange segments on top of the tuna.

In a small bowl whisk the extra virgin olive oil, 2 tablespoons of orange juice, the red wine vinegar, garlic, parsley, paprika, black pepper to taste and 1/2 teaspoon of salt. Pour over the salad, garnish with the olives and marinate for 30 minutes before serving.

Titbits
We're talking Spanish here – tuna, orange, olives and garlic. If you don't like the idea, move on to another recipe.

Pick up
Some decent red wine vinegar – and use it at every opportunity.

Essential
Spanish bottled tuna is in a class of its own. It costs an arm and a leg but it's worth it now and again. Spanish olive oil will give an authentic taste. Spanish paprika is particularly aromatic and smoky.

Alongside
It's easy to whip up a feast with tapas. Get in some decent Spanish wine, invite friends around to graze, send the new flamenco CDs spinning around and watch the action hot up!

Up front
You can cook the potatoes a day ahead if you wish, but line the container with absorbent kitchen paper to soak up moisture, and don't slice them until just before using.
If you really need to get organised, the oranges can be peeled and segmented a day ahead; keep them covered and refrigerated.

X-Factor
Another goodie: tuna provides an important opportunity to include selenium (practically an antioxidant in its own right) in the diet – it's also loaded with phosphorous and potassium and, when packed in oil, contains vitamin B12. Back to the selenium – which comes to us mostly via the soil and plants grown in it – some soils contain plenty of selenium, as in the USA, others not so much as in the UK, and some barely any, as in New Zealand. Tuna in oil has more selenium than tuna in brine or spring water and is an important ingredient to include regularly in the diet. However, not many manufacturers state which vegetable oil they use to pack the tuna. You can be sure that most will use the cheapest, most refined oil they can lay their hands on; always drain the tuna well before use.

Golden Glazed Poussins with Herbs

4 poussins
salt
2 tablespoons butter, melted
juice of 1 lemon
315ml (1¼ cups) light chicken stock
1 tablespoon each finely chopped flat-
  leafed parsley, mint and chives

Glaze
juice of 1 lemon
2 teaspoons caster sugar
¼ teaspoon paprika
salt
plenty freshly ground black pepper
knob of butter

SERVES 6

RINSE the poussins inside and out, then pat dry with absorbent kitchen paper. Season inside the cavities with a little salt. Secure the openings of the poussins with toothpicks, then put them in a smallish roasting tin. Brush them with melted butter, squeeze over the juice of the lemon and pour 1 cup of stock in the tin.

Roast in an oven preheated to 180°C (fanbake) for about 50 minutes, basting often, or until they are a rich golden brown and cooked through (scrape up the juices if they look like they are about to catch). Transfer the poussins to a chopping board and cut them in half through the breast using a sharp knife or poultry shears. Snip either side of the backbones and remove them. Put the halved poussins in a shallow dish which can go under the grill.

Squeeze the lemon over and sprinkle with the sugar and paprika, a little salt and black pepper (mix these together first). Drizzle with melted butter and cook under the grill until golden and sizzling. Skim the fat from the juices in the roasting tin and put the tin over a medium heat. Add the herbs and any juices which come out of the poussins while carving. Boil up the juices. Transfer the poussins to a heated serving platter and spoon over the juices. Serve immediately.

Titbits

These baby chickens are irresistible with their golden tasty skin and succulent flesh. I've always found that four poussins between six people is sufficient (some will have only half a poussin, and others will come back for another piece).

Pick up

Fresh, organically farmed free-range poussins if you can find them in your area.

Alongside

Try the poussins with steamed sticky-fluffy basmati rice, and a colourful combo of asparagus, snow peas, and yellow and red peppers stirfried together in a wok. Serve a fruity chardonnay with citrusy overtones to make the most of the buttery lemony poussins.

Up front

This is a great dish to do when you are having friends around. Roast the poussins and have them halved and ready to finish off under the grill before your friends arrive (the roasted poussins will be safe at room temperature for around 1½ hours), but squeeze the lemon juice over and season them just before you put them under the grill.

X-Factor

The skin on these poussins is meant to be eaten, so don't argue about this!

Hawke's Bay Salad

PEEL the pumkin, remove the seeds and cut the pumpkin into cubes. Put the pumpkin in a shallow tin (I use a Swiss roll tin), drizzle with a little extra virgin olive oil (use sparingly – it needs very little oil) and season with sea salt and black pepper. Bake in an oven preheated to 225°C (fanbake) for 15–20 minutes, or until lightly browned and just tender, turning once.

Put the onions in a small frying pan with 1 tablespoon of olive oil. Cook gently until wilted but not coloured. Arrange the hot pumpkin on a platter and put the hot onions on top. Cool for 10 minutes. Add the tomatoes, olives and basil leaves to the dish.

In a small bowl mix the rest of the oil with the vinegar, garlic and sea salt and black pepper to taste (about 1/2 teaspoon of salt, less if the feta is salty). Pour over the salad. Toss well, then crumble the feta on top. Add the toasted pumpkin seeds if using and toss very gently.

1.7kg firm-fleshed pumpkin, washed

5 tablespoons extra virgin olive oil

sea salt

freshly ground black pepper to taste

2 red onions, halved through the root end, then cut into slices through the root

150g (1 cup) sweet cherry tomatoes

100g (1/2 cup) black kalamata olives

15g (1/2 cup) basil leaves

1 tablespoon balsamic or red wine vinegar

2 cloves garlic, crushed

200g firm feta cheese, crumbled

5 tablespoons (1/4 cup) toasted salted pumpkin seeds, optional (see page 18)

SERVES 6-8

Titbits

This is a real 'sit up and take notice of me' kind of dish – colourful and bursting with taste. And the name? The inspiration came from a dish I ate in the Hawke's Bay in New Zealand.

Pick up

Organically grown pumpkin seeds. A good supplier of organic foods should be able to get you these. Pumpkin seeds are particularly creamy, delicious and nutritious when fresh and organically grown.

Essential

Firm pumpkin – purée is not the look you're aiming for here.

Alongside

Make it part of an all-vegetable meal and team it with a good spinach or green-leaf salad, and maybe grilled or baked mushrooms and, of course, good crusty bread. Alternatively, serve it with a lamb or chicken dish. And accompany with a glass of merlot or chardonnay.

Up front

You can assemble the salad an hour or so before serving; it is at its best while the pumpkin is still warm. The pumpkin seeds can be cooked several hours before required.

X-Factor

A sprinkling of seeds on top of salads does you a power of good. Pumpkin seeds (buy organic if you can) have a nutritious mix of minerals. They're great as a nibble with drinks too. Pumpkin itself is an excellent source of carotenoids (a class of antioxidants). Onions and garlic are valuable vegetables providing some defence against cancers. Think of the olive oil as delicious medicine (lowering cholesterol) and eat this salad with gusto!

Quick Couscous with Apricots, Almonds and Saffron

SOAK the apricots in very hot water for 1 hour.

Put the couscous in a bowl and pour the boiling water over it. Stir once, then cover and leave for 10 minutes. Fluff up with a fork, cover again and leave until cool.

Put the saffron strands in a small pan over a low heat for a few minutes until they smell aromatic and darken slightly. Tip them onto a plate. In the same pan put the butter. Add the almonds to the pan while the butter is sizzling. Cook gently until just starting to change colour, then add the crushed garlic. Cook for a few minutes more, stirring, until the garlic starts to turn golden. Turn off the heat.

Drain the apricots and mash the flesh. Put the lemon juice in a small bowl and add the salt, black pepper, olive oil, apricot purée and saffron. Mix this through the couscous along with some of the mint leaves. Tip the couscous onto a serving plate and spoon the buttery almonds and garlic over the top. Garnish with mint leaves and serve.

2 dried apricots
150g instant couscous
200ml boiling water
$^1/_2$ teaspoon saffron strands
knob of butter
30g ($^1/_4$ cup) slivered almonds
1 large clove garlic, crushed
$2^1/_2$ tablespoons lemon juice
$^1/_2$ teaspoon salt
freshly ground black pepper to taste
2 tablespoons extra virgin olive oil
tiny mint leaves

SERVES 6

Titbits
This is a quick and easy dish that works in all seasons.

Pick up
Instant couscous – it makes the job so easy.

Alongside
I'd go for lamb cutlets cooked on the barbecue or, for a bit more fun, panfried fish with Flame-roasted Tomato and Chilli Salsa (see page 91). This last combination may be a bit of a mix of cuisines, but it works on the plate and, more importantly, in the mouth. Choose a lively red wine, such as an inexpensive pinotage or a rosé.

X-Factor
You can make the dish several hours ahead, but add the mint at the last minute and tip the garlicky almonds on just before serving.

Green Beans with Shallots and Crispy Prosciutto

500g slim green beans, trimmed

salt

2 shallots, peeled and
    chopped (about $1/4$ cup)

1 clove garlic, crushed

large knob of butter

1 tablespoon olive oil

75g prosciutto

freshly ground black pepper to taste

SERVES 6

PLUNGE the beans into a saucepan of gently boiling salted water. Cook, uncovered, for 3–5 minutes, or until crisp-tender. Drain and refresh with a cup of cold water.

Put the shallots and garlic in a medium-sized pan with the butter. Set over a very gentle heat, cover with a lid, and cook until tender.

Just before serving, heat the oil in a small frying pan. When it is quite hot add the prosciutto pieces and cook them reasonably quickly until crisp. Transfer to a plate lined with absorbent kitchen paper and drain briefly.

Rewarm the shallot butter and add the green beans. Reheat carefully, tossing, and season with black pepper. When hot, turn the beans into a heated serving plate and top with the crisp prosciutto.

Titbits

This is the dish to think of when you want more than just a plate of green beans. The salty shards of sautéed prosciutto tickle the tastebuds.

Pick up

Crisp beans, not bendy beans that have lost all their snap.

Alongside

These beans are good with most meats and with all-vegetable meals, but they're especially delicious with a classic roast chicken flavoured with rosemary and either steamed kumara (sweet potatoes) or new potatoes.

Up front

The beans can be blanched and the shallot butter made an hour or so before serving. After draining the cooled beans, dry them with absorbent kitchen paper and keep them wrapped in the paper until required.

X-Factor

Beans contain fibre along with vitamins A and C and some of the B group, giving them a good antioxidant rating.

Butterflied Leg of Lamb with Coriander and Chilli

TRIM the fat off the meat but leave the skin on.

Squeeze the juice from the grated ginger and place it in a large shallow dish. Mix in the lime juice, honey, olive oil, salt and plenty of black pepper. Add the lamb and coat with the marinade. Cover and chill for at least 2 hours but up to 24, turning occasionally. Bring to room temperature before cooking.

To roast in the oven, heat a tablespoon of oil in a roasting tin in a very hot oven preheated to 220°C (fanbake). Lift the lamb out of the marinade and pat dry with absorbent kitchen paper. Remove the tin from the oven and put in the lamb, skin side uppermost. Roast for 45–60 minutes, basting with a little marinade once or twice.

To check whether the lamb is done to your liking, make a small incision through the meaty part after 45 minutes; remember that the lamb will continue to cook as it cools.

To barbecue, cook the lamb over a generous depth of glowing coals for 30–40 minutes, basting and turning occasionally. Check to see if it is cooked to your liking after 30 minutes.

When the lamb is sufficiently cooked, let cool for 12–15 minutes on a large plate, then make the dressing. Squeeze the juice from the grated ginger into a small bowl. Mix in the lime juice, salt, oil, sugar, garlic and chillies. Just before using, mix in the herbs.

Slice the lamb across the grain and arrange on a serving platter. Spoon the dressing over and serve. If you like, garnish with a few slices of fresh lime and 1–2 red chillies.

1 leg of lamb, 'butterflied'
knob of fresh ginger, grated
juice of 1 lime
1 tablespoon honey
2 tablespoons olive oil (a little extra if roasting the lamb)
1½ teaspoons salt
freshly ground black pepper to taste

Dressing
knob of fresh ginger, grated
juice of 1 lime
½ teaspoon salt
1 tablespoon extra virgin olive oil
2 teaspoons raw sugar
1 clove garlic, crushed
1–2 fresh hot red chillies, halved, deseeded and very finely chopped
1 tablespoon each chopped mint, coriander and basil

SERVES 6-8

Titbits

You may find it easier to put the marinade ingredients in a clean plastic bag with the lamb – it makes it very easy to turn the lamb – and saves on dishes (put the bag inside a dish). I prefer to cook this lamb over hot coals on a barbecue. The searing heat and smokiness give it an incomparable taste, but it can be cooked on a gas barbecue or in an oven. The result, whichever way you cook it, is tender meat, bursting with flavour. The lamb is thicker in parts. I like to cook it so that the thicker parts are cooked to medium-rare, which ensures that the rest will be cooked to medium. Put the thicker parts over the hottest part of the barbecue. Be very vigilant about the heat because the lamb can easily burn on the outside before it is cooked throughout; the best idea is to keep the heat constant, and to move the lamb further away from the source of heat if you need to.

Pick up

A boned leg of lamb, opened up like a butterfly – you'll probably have to go to a specialty butcher to get them to prepare it.

Essential

Quality lamb. This is not a recipe for hogget or mutton. I've already said it in this book – the best lamb comes from New Zealand.

Alongside

There is so much flavour from the barbecuing and the dressing that I favour playing down the accompaniments. A warm salad of new potatoes and a green salad will do the trick. It can work just as well with hot and fluffy rice and a regular salad, or an accompanying salad of cucumber and snow peas, or orzo (small rice-shaped pieces of pasta). Alternatively, accompany with a colourful healthy vegetable salad of a selection of the following: chick peas, new potatoes, roasted red and yellow peppers, sautéed courgettes (zucchini), sliced celery, sautéed button mushrooms, roasted or grilled spring onions, chunks of barbecued sweet corn, and fresh or slow-roasted tomatoes. There are many options for serving this!

I've enjoyed the lamb with a young chianti, a full-bodied cabernet sauvignon, and a shiraz – it depends on the mood.

Up front

The lamb can happily sit in its marinade for up to 24 hours until you get the urge to fire up the barbecue.

X-Factor

Lamb trimmed of fat is a fabulous meat, rich in iron, zinc and B vitamins. Just keep an eye on carcinogens (charring) forming on the outside of the lamb (if necessary, shave off blackened parts before serving).

Blackened Peppers with Hot-smoked Salmon and Fried Limes

2 red peppers (capsicums)
200g piece hot-smoked salmon
4 tablespoons extra virgin olive oil, plus a
    little for frying
2 limes, plus 2 tablespoons lime juice
chilli powder (ground dried chillies)
80g (4 cups) rocket leaves, trimmed
1/2 teaspoon salt
freshly ground black pepper to taste

SERVES 4 AS A STARTER

COOK the peppers directly over a gas flame until blackened, turning them with tongs (put them right in the flames). Alternatively, cook them in the flames of a barbecue, or on the rack in an oven preheated to 210°C (fanbake), turning them as they blacken (they'll take around 20 minutes). When all the outer skin is charred, transfer them to a plate and leave until cool. Peel off the blackened skins, rinsing your hands as you do this, but don't put the peppers under the running water (you'll rinse away flavour). Cut the peppers in half, remove the cores and seeds, reserving the juices, and cut the flesh into strips.

Remove the skin and bones from the salmon. Leave the fish in large flakes and transfer it to a container.

When ready to assemble, heat a small frying pan over a medium heat and add a smidgen of olive oil. Slice 2 limes and when the oil is hot add the slices of lime and cook for a few minutes each side until lightly browned. Transfer the lime slices to a plate and sprinkle with a little chilli powder.

Arrange the rocket leaves on a serving plate or on individual plates and top with chunks of salmon and strips of red pepper. Whisk the lime juice, olive oil, salt and black pepper together and pour over the salad. Decorate with the sliced limes.

Titbits

Fish can either be 'cold smoked' (such as salmon, which is cured, but not cooked, by faintly warm smoke) or 'hot smoked' – like most commercially smoked fish.
When correctly carried out, hot smoking involves preliminary cold smoking at around 10–30°C, then the temperature is raised and the food is briefly hot smoked. The low smoking temperature ensures that the smoke has time to fully permeate the fish, and so flavour it, and that sufficient moisture loss occurs, extending the keeping time of the fish. The final blast of heat forms a skin and improves the colour, as well as enhancing the surface flavour.
Salmon is particularly good hot smoked because of the high oil content which keeps it moist. I always wear food preparation gloves when preparing smoked salmon because the oil tends to penetrate the skin and it seems difficult to wash away the smell.
This is good as a starter, followed by a fish course.

Pick up

Fresh, juicy limes – buy four to be sure you've got enough.

Alongside

This is riesling territory, or serve a lightly oaked chardonnay.

Up front

The peppers can be roasted 24 hours before they are required. The salmon can be skinned and the bones removed the day before.

X-Factor

There are plenty of reasons to eat hot-smoked salmon – good B vitamins, niacin, phosphorous, potassium, selenium and iodine. Then there's omega-3 fatty acid, in which salmon is particularly rich. Omega-3 oils reduce the stickiness of blood and its tendency to clot, therefore lowering the risk of heart disease. And there is the health kick from peppers and rocket, making this a top dish.

Flame-roasted Tomato and Chilli Salsa

BLACKEN the tomatoes, chillies and garlic over a gas flame or in the charcoal embers of a barbecue. Start with the tomatoes and put them right in the flame of a gas element. Turn them with tongs as they blacken and char, then transfer to a plate as they are done. Do the chillies next, then the cloves of garlic (these are best done speared on metal skewers). Leave to cool.

The tendency is to peel away all the blackened skins; in the American south-west they don't bother with this too much as a little of the charred skin adds a welcome smoky bitterness. Put the tomatoes in a bowl and squeeze them to a pulp with your hands. Remove the stems from the chillies, then chop them finely and add to the tomatoes. Remove the burnt papery skins from the garlic, then cut the garlic into large pieces and pass them through a garlic crusher.

Add the garlic to the tomatoes and chillies, along with $1/4$ teaspoon of salt. Taste it – it should blow your socks off! You may need a little more salt, and you may need more garlic or chilli. And that's it.

6 medium vine-ripened tomatoes
2 hot green chillies
4 large cloves garlic, unpeeled
salt

SERVES 6

Titbits

If the tomatoes are small and difficult to balance on the element, put a cake rack on top of the element and put the tomatoes on this. Remove any greenery (the calyx) because it burns easily.

Pick up

Firm green chillies. A hot bite is part of this salsa's character. I'd look for a serrano or a jalapeño. If green chillies are not available, use fresh red chillies.

Essential

Icy beer to accompany.

Alongside

This is excellent with any barbecued meats, and with seafood, as well as with roast chicken (rub chicken skin with lime, sprinkle sea salt over, then roast), or with tacos filled with shredded lettuce, avocado and bacon, or sliced smoked pork.

Up front

The flame-roasted sauce will keep for a few days, covered and refrigerated.

X-Factor

Charred food is carcinogenic, though you're probably not going to die if you eat a crust of burnt toast or a few flecks of charred tomato skin occasionally. But if you do want to remove every trace of burnt skin, don't wash the tomatoes and chillies under running water because you'll wash off flavour; rinse your hands as you work and the blackened pieces of skin will wash off them.

Chicken Salad with Mint and Lemon Leaves

2 single chicken breasts, skin and any fat removed

knob of butter

sea salt

75g (½ cup) shelled peanuts (optional)

olive oil

½ telegraph cucumber (long, tender-skinned cucumber), peeled

10g (½ cup) mint leaves

2 carrots

75g (1 cup) fresh bean sprouts

4 juicy lemons

1 tablespoon caster sugar

6 fresh, unblemished lemon leaves, washed, dried and shredded very finely

1 fresh hot red chilli, seeds removed, sliced very finely

SERVES 4-6 AS A STARTER

PUT the chicken breasts in a small frying pan with a knob of just-melted butter. Cover with a lid and cook gently until the chicken is nearly cooked through. Season with sea salt, turn off the heat and keep covered for 15 minutes.

If using peanuts, put them in a shallow ovenproof dish. Toss with a little olive oil then roast in an oven preheated to 200°C (regular) for about 12 minutes, or until golden; check often and stir the peanuts often to encourage even browning. Remove from the oven and sprinkle well with sea salt. When cool, chop coarsely.

Cut the chicken breast into fine slivers and put them on a serving platter. Cut the cucumber in half lengthways, scoop out the seeds with a teaspoon, then cut into very thin half-moon slivers. Put these on top of the chicken. Scatter the mint leaves over. Peel the carrots into thin strips using a vegetable peeler and put these on top of the mint, along with the bean sprouts.

Mix the juice of the lemons with the sugar and ½ teaspoon of sea salt and add the slivered lemon leaves and chopped chilli. Just before serving, pour the dressing over the salad. Toss gently and scatter the chopped peanuts on top if using.

Titbits

Cooking the chicken gently like this produces delicate, succulent meat. Using lemon tree leaves came about because one day, lacking kaffir lime leaves, I substituted leaves from my lemon tree (having first checked that they weren't poisonous). I liked the result so much that I've stuck with them in the recipe. If you don't have a lemon tree, your neighbour may have one!

Don't cut back on the amount of lemon juice in this salad – it seems a lot, but the sharpness is tempered by the sugar. To strike the right balance, you definitely need a hot chilli.

Pick up

Good chicken breasts, not ones that are pumped with water to increase their weight. Free-range corn-fed organic chicken is best. Alternatively, use cooked chicken from a roast or another meal.

Essential

The lemon leaves – seriously.

Alongside

This is a light flavoursome dish, which could happily precede a fish dish, whole or fillets, or a prawn curry with sticky rice – that kind of thing. This will go beautifully with fruit-driven rieslings, colombard or chenin blanc.

Up front

The chicken can be cooked ahead; cool, cover and refrigerate until required.

The peanuts can be roasted and chopped several hours ahead. I'd prepare everything else as I assembled the dish.

X-Factor

Oh WOW, yes, this is brimming with goodness. The chicken is skinned and all fat removed, then it is cooked very gently in just a dab of butter (you could steam the chicken if you want to eliminate the butter). Peanuts add to the protein level in the dish as well as providing folate and B group vitamins. Then there are the nutrients from cucumber, carrots, bean sprouts and mint, along with a huge whack of vitamin C from the lemon juice.

Aubergine Toasties

DUNK the slices of aubergine in olive oil and cook on a hot barbecue plate until well browned. Transfer them to a large plate as they are done, and sandwich 2 slices of aubergine with 2 slices of mozzarella cheese in the middle.

Meanwhile, butter the bread on one side only, preparing enough for 6 sandwiches (12 slices of bread). When all the aubergine is cooked, scrape the barbecue plate as clean as possible and lower the heat.

If serving the salad ingredients, slice the tomatoes and dress the rocket leaves and basil with a little extra virgin olive oil, a few squirts of lemon juice, some sea salt and black pepper. Add a little crushed garlic and a dab of Dijon mustard if using.

Put half the slices of bread, buttered side down, on a board and spread with chutney. Put the aubergine and mozzarella bundles on the bread, season with sea salt and black pepper and put on the top slices of bread, buttered side up. Cook on a barbecue hot plate, heated to medium, until the bread is golden, then flip over and cook the second side. Transfer to a chopping board. Serve hot or hottish, cut into halves or triangles.

Titbits

When aubergine is cooked well on the barbecue, by that I mean cooked until it is tender, golden, slightly charred and smelling a little smoky, woody and caramelised, it is food for the gods. There's nothing worse than biting into uncooked aubergine – the astringency will make your teeth and tongue feel like you've just licked the carpet. This is not polite food – forget your manners, just bite through the melting threads of cheese and devour.

Pick up

Corn bread – you can use grainy bread instead, but it needs to be thickly sliced, as you would have it for toast. I love these toasties with chilli jam, but you can use any other tangy spread you happen to like which works well with aubergine, providing it doesn't add any richness (the aubergine is rich enough). For this reason stick with mozzarella cheese, which adds a melting quality but is low in fat. The quantities may well make more than 6 aubergine toasties – in which case, just butter some more bread!

Alongside

The toasties are delicious as they are, but a few slices of tomato tucked into the sandwiches along with some of the dressed rocket and basil leaves makes a tasty addition. Alternatively, serve the tomatoes and leaves separately. A wine? Chardonnay or a pinot noir.

Up front

You could cook the aubergine slices ahead of time, but assemble the toasties just before cooking them.

X-Factor

There's quite a bit of good stuff going on here with a range of vitamins and nutrients from aubergine, mozzarella cheese and corn bread or grainy bread. The salad garnish adds plenty of vitamin C. Well worth eating!

---

2 medium aubergines (eggplants), cut in slices 5mm thick
olive oil
150g fresh mozzarella bocconcini in whey, drained, patted dry and thinly sliced
soft butter
a loaf of corn bread, thickly sliced
chilli jam or fruity chutney
sea salt to taste
freshly ground black pepper to taste

Accompaniments (optional)
4 medium vine-ripened tomatoes
rocket leaves
basil
extra virgin olive oil
1/2 a juicy lemon
1 clove garlic, crushed
Dijon mustard (optional)

SERVES 6

stoking the fires

Roasted Pork Fillets with Apricots

2 medium-sized pork fillets (about 500g each)

150g ($^3/_4$ cup) dried apricots, soaked for several hours in $^2/_3$ cup hot water

freshly ground black pepper to taste

salt

a few sprigs of lemon thyme

2 tablespoons olive oil

60ml ($^1/_4$ cup) cream

SERVES 4

REMOVE any fat and silvery skin from the pork fillets. Lay the fillets on a board and slice down the centre of each, forming pockets. Drain the apricots and dry on absorbent kitchen paper (reserve the soaking liquid). Chop roughly. Grind black pepper over the cut surface of the fillets and sprinkle with salt. Scatter the lemon thyme over and put the apricots in the cavities. Make sure the apricots are enclosed in the cavities and tie gently with string.

Heat the olive oil in a heavy-based oval casserole, or one in which the fillets fit snugly, on a high element. When it is hot, add the fillets, slit side facing down, and brown quickly. Grind some black pepper over, turn over carefully with tongs, add a few sprigs of lemon thyme, then transfer, uncovered, to an oven preheated to 180°C (fanbake). Cook for 20 minutes.

Baste the meat twice during cooking, scraping up any glaze from the bottom to ensure it doesn't catch (add a few tablespoons of the apricot soaking liquid if it looks as if it will scorch). Cook for 10 minutes more, or until the fillets are cooked (the sliced meat should be rosy-coloured and juicy).

Remove the casserole from the oven, transfer the fillets to a chopping board and sprinkle with salt. Pour off any excess fat from the casserole and set it back over a medium heat, then pour in the cream. Bring to the boil, then lower the heat and cook for 2–3 minutes while slicing the meat. Remove the string from the meat, cut on the diagonal into thickish slices and arrange on a heated plate. Spoon the cream sauce over and serve immediately.

Titbits

This is a family favourite which I trot out at least once every winter to a thunderous applause (well, more than a grunt or two of appreciation).

Pick up

Fresh pork from a reliable butcher, organically raised if you can get it. Tangy apricots, which soften easily in water. The lemon thyme adds something very special to this dish, but it's not always available – so, if you have to, substitute thyme and lemon zest.

Alongside

I like these pork fillets with broccoli or broccolini, and a sweetish mash – parsnip and kumara (sweet potatoes) are good – to contrast with the tang of the apricots. I'd choose a luscious fragrant gewürztraminer to accompany the pork, or a floral limey riesling. If chardonnay's your bag, choose one with oodles of peachy-apricoty notes.

Up front

You could stuff and roll the fillets about an hour before cooking.

X-Factor

Pork is pork, but the lean cuts, such as pork fillet, have only a marginally higher fat content than beef. The meat is full of the B vitamin family.

Dark apricots that are not treated with sulphur to preserve their colour are particularly nutritious.

Rabbit in Pinot

1 rabbit (about 1.25kg), trimmed of fat and
   cut into small joints (ask your butcher to
   do it)
2 red peppers (capsicums)
2 tablespoons butter
1 tablespoon oil
15 small pickling onions, peeled, but leave
   the root intact
200g bacon, diced
2 tablespoons plain flour
250ml pinot noir
$1/4$ teaspoon salt
freshly ground black pepper to taste
3 fresh bay leaves
12 fresh sage leaves
small clump fresh thyme
1 tablespoon chopped flat-leafed parsley

SERVES 4

REMOVE any lumps of fat from the rabbit and check for any bone fragments.

Cook the peppers directly over a gas flame until blackened, turning them with tongs (put them right in the flames). Alternatively, cook them in the flames of a barbecue, or on the rack in an oven preheated to 210°C (fanbake), turning them as they blacken (they'll take around 20 minutes). When all the outer skin is charred, transfer them to a plate and leave until cool. Peel off the blackened skins, rinsing your hands as you do this, but don't put the peppers under the running water (you'll rinse away flavour). Cut the peppers in half, remove the cores and seeds and cut the flesh into thick strips.

Put a heavy-based casserole over a medium heat to warm. Put in the butter and oil. Add the onions and cook for about 10 minutes, until starting to brown, then add the bacon and cook until crisp, stirring often. Transfer to a side plate.

Brown the rabbit joints in the casserole (best done in batches), transferring them to the side plate as they are done; let them take on a deep brown colour because it develops flavour. Sprinkle with the flour and blend it in with a metal spoon. Return the bacon and onions to the pan (leave the rabbit on the plate), and pour the wine in. Bring to the boil, add the salt, some pepper, the bay leaves, sage leaves, thyme and the rabbit joints. Cover with a lid and braise in an oven preheated to 140°C (fanbake) for $1^{1}/_{2}$ hours.

Add the peppers to the casserole just before serving. Sprinkle with parsley and serve.

Titbits

Caramelised onions, sweet savoury bacon, plenty of herbs, intense wine flavours, and roasted peppers, all in the saucepan with a bunny! Get over the bunny thing, and discover rabbit if you haven't already. This is one of my best dishes in a long time. Watch the bones though, they shatter more easily than chicken bones; run your fingers over the cut pieces to check for any bone fragments (rinse the rabbit with cold water if there are any). Cooking peppers over the gas flame gives them a magnificent flavour and they remain crunchy.

Essential

A bottle of New Zealand pinot noir. Really. The dish just won't be the same with anything else.

Alongside

It's time to make a big creamy but light potato purée — remember to use hot milk in the purée because anything which is warm will hold more air than anything which is not warm, resulting in a lighter purée. And hot milk stops the potatoes turning gluggy (cold liquids added to starchy ingredient – rice, pasta, potatoes – make them tacky). I'd also serve some broccoli, broccolini, bok choy or lightly steamed cabbage to balance the meal.

Up front

The whole thing can be cooked ahead, but add the peppers just before serving.

X-Factor

Rabbit is a low-fat source of protein. It's easy to overcook it and make it dry, so some fat has to be added when cooking to prevent this and make it palatable. Think of the B6 and B12 vitamins it brings to the diet, and the amazing properties of red peppers (antioxidants, a big whack of vitamin C, folate, etc). That's enough reason to eat and enjoy this dish.

Witloof, Red Apple and Pine Nut Salad

TRIM the ends of the witloof, then gouge out the cores and remove any damaged leaves. Slice into chunks, separating the leaves, and put in a salad bowl (alternatively, separate the witloof into small leaves).

Put the pine nuts in a small, lightly oiled frying pan. Set over a low to medium heat and cook, shaking the pan often, until lightly browned. Set aside.

Wash and dry the apples. Cut into thin slivers and drop into a bowl with the lemon juice. Toss the apple slices in the juice, then add to the salad bowl. Scatter with the mint or chives, grind on black pepper, sprinkle with salt and pour the oil over. Toss very well. Scatter the pine nuts on top and serve.

6 firm witloof (chicory)
3 tablespoons pine nuts
2 tablespoons extra virgin olive oil (choose a fruity type), plus a little extra for oiling the pan
2 red apples
1 tablespoon lemon juice
1 tablespoon snipped chopped mint or snipped chives
freshly ground black pepper to taste
$1/4$ teaspoon salt

SERVES 6 AS A STARTER

Titbits

The crisp, fleshy, juicy stems of witloof have a hint of bitterness which adds interest to the palate, especially when eaten with something sweet or bland. This is an unbelievably crunchy, crisp, fresh salad.

Pick up

If witloof is exposed to the light it will become very bitter – that's why it should be sold wrapped in light-resistant paper. Choose blemish-free crisp apples; gala apples are perfect.

Essential

Make sure the pine nuts you buy are fresh – rancid pine nuts will ruin the dish. Store pine nuts in the freezer because they go rancid very quickly.

Up front

The problem with toasting the pine nuts ahead of time is that you'll be tempted to nibble on them. In no time at all the pile of pine nuts will be reduced from 3 tablespoons to 1 (in other words, do extra!). Otherwise, assemble the dish just before serving.

X-Factor

This is a plate of goodness – vitamin C from apples and lemon and good quantities of vitamin A, calcium, iron and potassium from witloof. Pine nuts, although high in fat (it's mostly polyunsaturated fat, not saturated) are a good food source, having a range of nutrients and considerable protein. If you're vegetarian, try to include them in your diet on a regular basis.

Braised Duckling with Green Olives

REMOVE as much fat as possible from the duck legs.

Choose a casserole big enough to fit the duck legs in one layer. Put it over a medium heat and, when hottish, add the butter. Brown the duck legs slowly on both sides (allow 15–20 minutes for this; lower the temperature after the first few minutes' cooking). Transfer to a plate, then pour off most of the fat, leaving just a tablespoonful of it in the casserole.

Add the onion to the casserole, cover with a lid, and cook gently until tender. Add the garlic, paprika and bay leaves. Cook for a minute or two, then pour the sherry in. Let the sherry bubble up, then add the stock. Bring back to the boil, then return the duck legs to the casserole, seasoning them with salt and black pepper. Put a lid on the casserole and transfer it to an oven preheated to 175°C (fanbake). Cook for 1 hour, turning the duck legs once.

Transfer the duck legs to a heated dish and put the casserole over a medium heat. Skim off any fat. Add the olives and tomatoes to the dish, check for seasoning, then spoon the sauce over the duck joints. Serve immediately.

4 duck legs

knob of butter

1 large onion, sliced

2 cloves garlic, crushed

1 teaspoon smoked hot Spanish paprika

5 fresh bay leaves

60ml ($1/4$ cup) dry sherry

375ml ($1 1/2$ cups) chicken stock

$1/4$ teaspoon salt

freshly ground black pepper to taste

12 large green olives, drained

2 large tomatoes, skinned, deseeded and sliced

SERVES 4

Titbits

This is a fantastic way to cook duck, rendering it fork-tender and full of lusty flavours.

Pick up

Try to find Spanish Queen or Italian Cerignolo olives.

Essential

Smoked paprika combined with good firm green olives gives this dish its character. If you use squishy-soft green olives and old musty paprika you've had in the pantry for 2 years, it'll be a disappointment.

Alongside

I particularly like this with steamed baby bok choy – they've got just the right crunch and juice – but tight little Brussels sprout buds and verdant broccoli florets also work, and a good potato mash acts as a pillow for all the rich juices. A suitable wine? I'd stick to Spanish flavours, perhaps a tempranillo, or opt for a pinot noir.

Up front

Duck reheats well, and this dish is no exception. So make it the day before, or on the morning you plan to serve it, cool it, refrigerate it, then warm it through slowly in the oven.

X-Factor

It is healthy because I've given every opportunity to rid the duck legs of fat, and lean duck meat has plenty of B vitamins and nutrients – of course you could always conserve the fat and fry up some potatoes in it the next day (they're ridiculously fattening and bad for you, but they are sooo delicious!).

Lamb Cutlets Catalan-style

2 eggs

¹/₂ teaspoon salt

75g (³/₄ cup) finely ground dry breadcrumbs

6 tablespoons freshly grated parmesan (parmigiano reggiano) cheese

1kg Frenched lamb cutlets

olive oil and clarified butter

150g (³/₄ cup) black olives, stoned and chopped

freshly ground black pepper to taste

2 tablespoons lemon juice

1 tablespoon chopped fresh marjoram or a few pinches of dried oregano

SERVES 4-6

BREAK the eggs onto a plate and add the salt. Beat well with a fork. Mix the breadcrumbs and parmesan cheese together on a second plate. Coat the cutlets with the beaten egg, letting the excess drip off, then coat them with the flavoured crumbs. Stack on a tray between layers of waxed paper.

Heat 2 tablespoons of oil with 2 tablespoons of clarified butter in a heavy-based frying pan over a medium heat. When hot, put in enough cutlets to cover the bottom of the pan without crowding it. Cook for 4–5 minutes until golden, then cook the second side. Keep warm, uncovered, in a low oven while cooking the other cutlets.

When all the cutlets are cooked, pour off all but 2 tablespoons of the oily sediment in the pan. If the pan is very hot, let it cool down briefly before proceeding. Add the olives and cook for 1–2 minutes, then grind on plenty of black pepper and pour the lemon juice in. Let the olive mixture get hot, then stir the marjoram in. Spoon around, not over, the cutlets and serve immediately.

Titbits

I've been making these cutlets for years and I still get excited about them: tender, golden and crisp, with the fresh taste of lemon cutting through the full fruity taste of olives and musky notes of marjoram.

Essential

If you attempt this recipe with hefty fatty chops, you won't thank me. You need thin lamb cutlets, well trimmed.

Alongside

Any of the starchy things – potato purée, couscous, burghul – will work with these cutlets, and green beans or courgettes. Alternatively, something like caponata (Sicilian aubergine stew) or ratatouille will work a treat.

Up front

The cutlets can be coated 2–3 hours before cooking (wrap them and keep them refrigerated), but fry them just before serving. Serve a well-rounded cabernet sauvignon alongside – the tannins in the wine will be softened by the sweet fat in the lamb.

X-Factor

A lack of iron lowers physical performance and affects mental powers too, such as the ability to concentrate. Lamb is an excellent source of iron and it also contains B vitamins. Serving iron-rich meats like lamb or beef at the same meal as a cereal (such as bread or rice) allows the body to absorb the iron more readily. Vitamin C also helps iron absorption.

Roasted Chicken with Sage and Orange

PUT 2–3 pieces of the orange rind, a large sprig of sage, 1 clove of garlic and ¼ teaspoon of salt inside the cavity of the chicken. Cut the other clove of garlic into four slivers. Slip a few leaves of sage, 2 pieces of orange rind and the garlic slivers between the breast skin and breast meat of the chicken.

Tie the chicken legs together with string, hooking the string around the parson's nose to keep the cavity closed.

Set a large heavy-based casserole over a medium heat and add the butter. When it is hot, put in the chicken, breast down. Brown gently; if the casserole gets too hot, the butter and chicken may burn. Turn the chicken over with tongs and brown the other side. Add the rest of the sage leaves (reserve a sprig for garnishing), and the orange rind, sprinkle with salt, then pour in the wine and ½ cup of stock.

Cover the casserole and transfer to an oven preheated to 180°C (fanbake). Cook for 30 minutes, remove the casserole from the oven, take off the lid and baste well. Return to the oven without the lid and cook for a further 45–60 minutes, or until golden and cooked through. Baste the chicken several times during cooking, scraping up any caramelising juices (add more stock or a little water if necessary, to stop the juices catching).

Transfer the chicken to a board and let it rest for 15–30 minutes, loosely covered with greaseproof paper. Attend to the juices in the casserole. Tilt the casserole and scoop off any fat. Add the remaining ¼ cup of stock and boil the juices until reduced and syrupy. Add the olives and let them warm through.

Carve the chicken into joints, spoon on the juices (reheat if necessary) and garnish with sage.

thinly peeled rind of 1 orange (scrape off any white pith with a knife)
6 large sprigs fresh sage
2 large cloves garlic
salt
1 free-range corn-fed organic chicken, about 1.4kg), rinsed inside and out and patted dry with absorbent kitchen paper
large knob of clarified butter
125ml (½ cup) dry white wine
190ml (¾ cup) light chicken stock, or more
100g (½ cup) black olives, stoned

SERVES 4–6

Titbits

The perfume of orange rind, the earthy taste of olives and potent aroma of sage give this chicken an exotic fragrance and flavour.

Pick up

I know it's tempting to buy olives already stoned – DON'T! They've been heat-treated to extract the stones, and a considerable amount of their flavour and oil is removed in the process.

Essential

The chicken must be organic and fresh. Use clarified butter because it doesn't burn as easily as butter.

Alongside

Serve with a mash of potatoes whipped with butter, hot milk, salt and snipped chives, and some good snappy green beans, or quinoa. Alternatively, serve it with couscous (flavour it with fresh mint, a touch of paprika or chilli, lemon juice, tiny currants and toasted slivered almonds), and quickly blanched sugar snap peas or snow peas (mangetout). A merlot with sweet plummy fruit flavours will work wonders with this, or stick with a safe citrusy chardonnay.

Up front

The chicken can be prepared for the oven ahead of time (keep covered and refrigerated), and the olives stoned (keep covered at room temperature). The chicken can be served at room temperature if that suits the occasion.

X-Factor

You'll find the chicken skin irresistible – it's imbued with the flavours of orange, garlic and sage – and is all golden and gorgeous. Do penance the night after and have a lettuce leaf for dinner.

Chicken Breasts with Marsala and Kalamata Olives

4 single chicken breasts, skin and fat removed

3 tablespoons plain flour

3 tablespoons olive oil

1–2 tablespoons butter

salt to taste

freshly ground black pepper to taste

1 tablespoon extra virgin olive oil

4 cloves garlic, finely chopped

50g (¼ cup) kalamata olives, stoned and chopped

1 tablespoon fresh marjoram leaves or ½ tablespoon dried marjoram

2 medium vine-ripened tomatoes, diced (squeeze out as many seeds as possible)

60ml (¼ cup) dry marsala (I used Pellegrino Marsala Fine)

SERVES 4

CUT each chicken breast into three pieces of even thickness (cut off the tail-end as one piece, then slit the other piece through the middle). Coat the pieces with flour, dusting off the excess.

Set a frying pan over a medium heat. When hot add 2 tablespoons of olive oil then a good knob of butter. Put in the pieces of chicken while the butter is sizzling. Cook the breasts for about 5 minutes a side, or until golden and cooked through.

Transfer the chicken pieces to a heated plate when done. If you need to cook the chicken in two batches, keep the first lot warm in a heated oven, then add another tablespoon of oil to the pan and cook the remaining chicken pieces in the same way. When all the chicken is cooked, season it with salt and black pepper.

Let the pan cool a little then, if the pan is dry, add the extra virgin olive oil (if there is oily residue, you won't need it). Add the garlic, cook for a few minutes, then add the olives, marjoram and tomatoes. Cook for 2–3 minutes, then pour in the marsala and let the mixture bubble up. Pour it over the chicken breasts and serve immediately.

Titbits

Overcooked chicken breast is tough. The aim is to get it just cooked through, so it's safe to eat but still juicy and a pale rosy colour inside; the meat will continue cooking with the residual heat as it stands (this is how you achieve juicy succulent chicken). And free-range corn-fed organic chicken is best.

Pick up

Good marsala. Once it is opened, it lasts several weeks before it starts to lose its freshness, so plan to whip up a round of zabaglione and to drink a few warming glasses of it some time soon after the bottle is opened.

Alongside

It's delicious with sautéed mushrooms and a bowl of broccoli showered in freshly grated parmesan (parmigiano reggiano) cheese. The chicken can take a red wine because of the depth of flavour from the marsala. A cabernet sauvignon with sweet berry-fruit flavours or perhaps a lighter chianti will make great match-ups.

Up front

Prepare the chicken and keep it covered and in the fridge until required. Stone and chop the olives and peel the garlic a day ahead if need be (don't chop the garlic until cooking the chicken breasts).

X-Factor

The chicken skin has been removed, getting rid of a lot of fat, but olive oil and butter help the chicken breasts to colour and develop flavour. Increase the nutrients of the meal by serving with a selection of vegetables.

Panfried Chicken Breasts with Tarragon and Cream

4 single chicken breasts, skin and fat
removed
1 tablespoon olive oil
1½ tablespoons butter
fresh tarragon (if not available, use dried
tarragon)
salt
freshly ground black pepper to taste
60ml (¼ cup) chicken stock
60ml (¼ cup) cream

SERVES 4

CHOOSE a heavy-based frying pan large enough to hold the chicken breasts and heat it over a medium heat; the pan should have a lid, or improvise with a large heavy-duty china plate. Add the oil, then the butter. Put the chicken breasts in the pan with what was the skin side facing down, while the butter is foaming. Let them brown for about 5 minutes, loosen them from the bottom of the pan and check on the colour; they should be a good golden colour.

Put a few sprigs of tarragon or some dried tarragon leaves on the breasts, then turn them over and put the lid on. Lower the heat a little. Cook them gently for about 8 minutes, depending on the thickness of the breasts. Remove the lid and let them continue browning for a few minutes. If in doubt over whether they are cooked, make an incision into one of them in the thickest part; it should be faintly pink and juicy (it will continue to finish off cooking with residual heat as it stands).

Transfer the chicken breasts to a heated platter and season well with salt and black pepper. Let the pan cool for a few minutes, pour off any fat and add the chicken stock. Scrape up any bits and pieces stuck on the pan, then swirl in the cream and add some more fresh tarragon, if using. Let the mixture bubble and reduce a little, and when it is creamy pour it over the chicken breasts. Serve immediately.

Titbits

Chicken and tarragon make an exceptional twosome. Yes, chicken and rosemary is a head-turner, too, but the fresh anise flavour of tarragon somehow makes chicken taste much more interesting.

Pick up

Fresh tarragon, if possible. I much prefer this dish with fresh French tarragon but it's a difficult herb to grow (for me at any rate) and I occasionally resort to dried tarragon. I dry the tarragon on the stalks, leaving them at room temperature until they're thoroughly dry, then pack them loosely in a glass jar (it's nearly as good as with fresh tarragon). Obviously choose fabulous free-range corn-fed organic chicken breasts that have been lovingly nurtured.

Alongside

I'd opt for steamed kumara (sweet potatoes), or a mix of long grain rice and wild rice, and leeks to balance the richness. The dish calls for a wine with some acid – probably a fruit-driven chardonnay with citrus overtones, maybe some biscuit notes – a wine which will add another dimension to the flavours without adding further richness.

Up front

This is a relatively pacy dish to put together. I don't advise cooking the breasts then reheating them; they are at their most succulent when they are freshly cooked.

X-Factor

The velvety texture of cream gives this dish a high rating in the pleasure stakes – but at a cost. You can make it without the cream, but it just won't be the same. Concentrate instead on the chicken skin – you dumped it in the bin so that's some fat you won't be consuming (chicken is a good low-fat source of protein, providing the skin is not eaten). Enjoy it!

Rabbit with Three Herbs and Mustard

SMEAR the rabbit joints with the mustard, then dust them with 1 tablespoon of the flour.

Heat a large heavy-based casserole over a medium heat and pour in one tablespoon of olive oil, then drop in the butter. When the butter is sizzling, add half the rabbit joints to the casserole and brown on both sides. Transfer to a plate and repeat the process with the rest of the rabbit joints.

Add the remaining oil to the casserole, along with the onion. Cover the casserole with a lid and cook gently until tender and golden. Add the garlic and cook for 2 minutes more.

Sprinkle the remaining flour over, then stir in the stock and add the tomato purée, herbs, salt and black pepper. Bring to the boil, then return the rabbit joints to the casserole. Cover with a lid and transfer the casserole to an oven preheated to 180°C (fanbake) and cook for about 40–60 minutes or until tender, turning once during cooking.

1 rabbit (about 1.25kg), trimmed of fat and cut into small joints (ask your butcher to do it)
2 teaspoons Dijon mustard
2 tablespoons plain flour
$2^1/_2$ tablespoons olive oil
small knob of butter
1 large onion, finely chopped
2 cloves garlic, crushed
400ml chicken stock
1 tablespoon tomato purée (concentrate)
1 tablespoon chopped rosemary
1 tablespoon chopped thyme
2 bay leaves, halved
$^1/_2$ teaspoon salt
freshly ground black pepper to taste

SERVES 4-6

Titbits

There are several points to remember when preparing and cooking rabbit.
Firstly, the bones do not break as cleanly as those of chicken, they tend to shatter so you can end up with little fragments of bone throughout the flesh if you're not careful. When jointing a rabbit, slice through the ball and socket joints, and use poultry shears for cutting through bones. Your butcher can usually make a clean job of it.
Rabbit flesh is a little firmer in texture than that of chicken. There is less fat through the flesh. Unlike chicken, it doesn't become tenderer with longer cooking.
Once it's cooked, it's ready!

Pick up

Farm-reared rabbits, not wild ones because the meat is more dependably tender.

Alongside

Serve with a bowl of whipped potato purée, or a bowl of crushed jersey bennes potatoes or other new freshly dug potatoes with lumps of butter! (To prepare the jersey bennes, steam or boil them until tender, drain, cool a little, then turn into a serving bowl. Crush with a fork, sprinkle with salt and dot with butter.) For a green vegetable, I'd keep it simple, remembering the season, and go for lightly steamed cabbage (sliced, and cooked for just 3 minutes in the saucepan with a knob of butter so that it keeps its colour and crunch – and vitamins!), or leeks, or stewed peas (Yes!

Stewed! Mix frozen peas with onion and garlic softened in butter, add little water and some salt and black pepper. Cover with a lid and cook gently for 20 minutes. Add some basil or thyme before serving.).
To drink? A big rich chardonnay, or a merlot or pinot noir.

Up front

The rabbit can be cooked ahead, providing it is reheated gently.

X-Factor

I have never understood why some people can happily tuck into chicken but the merest mention of rabbit makes them go peculiar. I'm not going to dwell on that. But I am going to say that rabbit has less fat than chicken yet more flavour, and it's a very low-fat source of protein. It has a good mix of nutrients too, including niacin, B6, B12, potassium and phosphorous. What does all that stuff do? Just think energy and healthy blood cells and nerves.

A Really Good Spinach Salad

6 medium free-range eggs, at room
   temperature
100g pancetta or 150g streaky bacon
150g very fresh baby spinach leaves
3 tablespoons extra virgin olive oil
1 tablespoon red wine or sherry vinegar
sea salt
freshly ground black pepper to taste
1 large clove garlic, crushed
1 tablespoon olive oil
250g very fresh button mushrooms, wiped
   and thickly sliced
2 tablespoon snipped chives

SERVES 6

COOK the eggs first. Prick the rounded end of the eggs with a dressmaking pin to make a little hole for the air to come out as the contents of the eggs expand in the heat (this stops the shells cracking and uncooked egg bursting out). Lower them into a saucepan of gently boiling water and cook for 8 minutes. If you use medium eggs and have them at room temperature before cooking, this should produce beautifully cooked eggs with creamy, soft yolks. Drain, let the cold tap flow over the eggs in the saucepan for a few minutes, then shell them. Set aside.

Grill the pancetta or bacon. Put the spinach leaves in a big salad bowl. In a small bowl whisk together the extra virgin olive oil, vinegar, 1/2 teaspoon of sea salt, black pepper and garlic.

Heat a medium frying pan over a high heat. When the pan is hot add the olive oil and get that very hot. Drop in the mushrooms and cook very quickly, tossing often, until a rich golden colour. Season with sea salt and black pepper. Add the chives to the dressing, whisk again, and pour it over the salad. Toss well. Slice the eggs and add to the salad bowl. Toss gently. Pour in the mushrooms, toss and garnish with bacon. Serve immediately.

Titbits

I'm an absolute hater of frilly lettuce – you know that 'lollo rosso' stuff which is limp in the mouth and pretty bland to eat – so it doesn't make it into my salad bowl. I also hate pea-shoots – those long pieces of fibre that get caught in your teeth – there's just no way you can eat them politely. But you can put whatever you like in your salad bowl, the key being to use a variety of colours and textures and to provide juiciness and taste. A little finely chopped shallot, a dab of Dijon mustard, grated zest of a lemon, a handful of fresh herbs – mint is particularly good in winter – can make a difference to a salad. Most greens benefit from good oil, a miserly splash of decent wine vinegar, a bigger pinch of salt then you think you'll need and a good grind of fresh pepper. Spinach can be quite chalky in the mouth and needs plenty of dressing to make it palatable. Mixing it with a juicy salad item such as witloof is another good ploy.

Pick up

Very fresh spinach – don't make this a home for wilted blackening spinach leaves. And button mushrooms in pristine condition are easy enough to find, so don't settle for soggy ones. Pancetta has great flavour, but it's twice the price of bacon! If you are grilling pancetta, take care because it cooks very quickly and can burn easily.

Alongside

I'd serve this as part of a vegetable meal (omit the bacon or pancetta if you're a vegetarian), with a crunchy-crust jacket-baked potato or kumara (sweet potato) for a mid-week easy dinner.

Up front

The eggs can be cooked and cooled, the bacon or pancetta cooked, the spinach washed and the dressing assembled an hour or two before required.

X-Factor

I don't want to burst your bubble, but cooked spinach is better for you than raw, because the carotenoids (a class of antioxidants) are absorbed better. But that aside, fresh spinach still delivers good nutrients. Garlic, mushrooms and eggs help make this a good-for-you salad.

Witloof Salad with Walnuts and Black Olives

1 juicy orange
3 tablespoons walnut oil
1 tablespoon lemon juice
a few pinches of sea salt
freshly ground black pepper to taste
4 witloof (chicory)
25g (¼ cup) coarsely chopped walnuts
100g (½ cup) dried black olives
1 tablespoon marjoram leaves

SERVES 4

PEEL the orange with a serrated knife, removing all the white pith, then cut in between the segments to release the orange fillets. Put these in a side bowl, and squeeze any juice in the membrane into a salad bowl. Mix in the walnut oil, lemon juice, sea salt and black pepper.

Trim the ends of the witloof, then gouge out the cores and remove and discard any damaged leaves. Peel off the leaves, putting them in the bowl with the dressing. Add the walnuts, olives, orange segments and marjoram. Toss and serve.

Titbits

This salad is exceptional. Just think – juicy oranges cutting through the earthy taste of olives, with sweet creamy walnuts and musky notes of marjoram nestled on pristine witloof leaves. It's quietly orgasmic.

Pick up

Greek Thassos olives from the island of Thassos. Picked when fully ripe, they're cured in sea salt, then washed with fresh water, coated with a little olive oil and layered with oregano. Their flavour is of beautifully ripe olives, earthier though not as salty as regular olives. The taste is curious too, and you'll either love them (I'm addicted) or loathe them (use regular olives in that case).
Never buy witloof that has been exposed to the light for a long period because it turns bitter. You might be lucky enough to find red witloof – the leaves are a little furrier than the white variety and are perhaps sweeter to taste; the two look amazing mixed together.

Essential

Fresh, creamy walnuts. Bitter walnuts ruin any dish they are added to.

Alongside

Either serve this as an unusual starter, or team it with roasted or barbecued chicken.

Up front

If you need to, peel the orange ahead of time and cut it into fillets; it'll hold covered in the fridge overnight. Otherwise, assemble everything when it's required.

X-Factor

All nuts should be fresh – rancid nuts are toxic. Walnuts are packed with goodies – B1, B6, folate vitamin E – along with several minerals. Witloof has good amounts of vitamin A, calcium, iron, fibre and potassium. This salad is well worth eating.

Rack of Lamb with Cardamom and Fennel Seed

2 full racks of young lamb, about 450g
  each, or 4 racks with 4 cutlets each
5 pods of cardamom, seeds only, lightly
  crushed
2 tablespoons Dijon mustard
1 tablespoon scented honey
1 tablespoon lemon juice
freshly ground black pepper to taste
30g (½ cup) fresh breadcrumbs
grated zest of ½ lemon
1 teaspoon fennel seeds
2 tablespoons olive oil, plus a little more
  for drizzling
3 tablespoons freshly grated parmesan
  (parmigiano reggiano) cheese
salt

SERVES 4

PREPARE the lamb racks first, removing excess fat and silverskin if necessary. Mix the cardamom seeds, mustard, honey and lemon juice in a small bowl with a grind of black pepper.

Mix the breadcrumbs, lemon zest and fennel seeds with the olive oil and parmesan. Lightly season the lamb racks with salt and black pepper and wrap the bone tips with aluminium foil to prevent them burning. Put the racks in an oiled shallow ovenproof dish, skin side facing up. Spread the honey mixture over the lamb, then press the crumb mixture on.

Cook the lamb racks in an oven preheated to 210°C (fanbake) for 15 minutes for pink juicy lamb; don't overcook (allow an extra 5 minutes if you want them more cooked). Transfer the racks to a chopping board and sprinkle generously with salt. Let them rest for 5–7 minutes, then slice into cutlets.

Titbits

Cardamom is one of the most expensive spices. When crushed it releases its heady camphor-like fragrance and imparts a bitter-sweet taste to food. It can become highly addictive! Fennel adds the fresh taste of anise to the mix.
You may be surprised to see that I have combined these spices with parmesan cheese, mustard and lemon – just try it, it's a stunner!

Pick up

Look for green cardamom pods – white ones have been bleached. Don't bother with ground cardamom because it loses its strength very quickly once ground. Choose a floral or scented honey to match the strength of the other seasonings. If the honey is firm, loosen it in a microwave for a few seconds, or in a small bowl in warm water. I buy the lamb racks with the fat removed and peel off the silverskin.

Essential

Perfect lamb. There's no point in doing this with anything but young, tender and juicy lamb.

Alongside

A little couscous or quinoa would do the trick, and maybe some baby bok choy (they must be very small) if you can get them. Otherwise, go for stirfried yellow and green scallopini or roasted asparagus. And merlot will make a delicious partner.

Up front

The lamb can be prepared in advance, as can the other ingredients, but don't put the crumb mixture on the lamb until just before cooking (the crumbs can go soggy).

X-Factor

The exotic mix of cardamom, fennel and scented honey should bring about a little 'ooh-ing and ahh-ing'.

Baked Spicy Ricotta with Fresh Mint

LINE a shallow ovenproof dish with a piece of baking paper, extending the ends a little to make it easy to remove the cooked ricotta. Put the ricotta in the dish and crumble the dried oregano and chillies over the top. Drizzle with a little olive oil.

Bake in an oven preheated to 220°C for around 20 minutes, or until the ricotta has started to colour on the top and around the edges.

Have ready in a small bowl the olives, freshly ground black pepper, a few pinches of sea salt, the lemon zest, and a handful of mint leaves mixed with 3 tablespoons extra virgin olive oil. Spoon the olive dressing over the ricotta and garnish with caper berries.

1kg (in a round shape) fresh ricotta
1–2 tablespoons dried oregano
4 tiny dried bird's eye chillies, crushed
extra virgin olive oil
50g (¼ cup) kalamata or small niçoise
   olives
freshly ground black pepper to taste
sea salt
grated zest of 1 lemon
small mint leaves
caper berries

SERVES 10 (OR HALVE THE MIXTURE FOR 5-6)

Titbits

This is a really impressive starter which works well as part of a buffet or drinks party. You'll need plates and forks unless it's for an outdoor gathering where you could get away with scooping everything onto bread. Cooking the ricotta dries it a little, making it firmer and easy enough to slice, although it remains moist. Don't stint on the accompaniments - it can take lots of flavourings and oil, and plenty of bread.

Essential

You'll need to order the authentic ricotta from a cheesemaker, as what is usually sold as ricotta is packed into small tubs, not made in a mould and sold in a round unmoulded shape. It's worth getting the real thing.

Alongside

Have sea salt and extra virgin olive oil on the table for serving, and accompany the ricotta with crusty ciabatta bread and a salad of vine-ripened tomatoes and rocket.

Up front

The ricotta can be prepared ahead for the oven, but don't drizzle with oil until you are ready to bake it. After baking, it keeps well at room temperature for an hour or two. If you want to serve it hot, don't garnish with salad or it will wilt; serve it separately.

X-Factor

Ricotta has a fat content of around 11%. Cream cheese has around 37-75%, butter around 80% and cheddar around 35%. You can see where it fits in the scale. Have seconds.

snuggle-up suppers

Pumpkin and Roasted Garlic Risotto

1 head of garlic

olive oil

750g firm-fleshed pumpkin

75g butter

1 tablespoon chopped rosemary spikes

1.3 litres chicken stock

1 small onion, finely chopped

125ml (1/2 cup) dry white wine

400g (about 1¾ cups) Italian rice –
   arborio, vialone nano, carnaroli

1/4 teaspoon salt

freshly ground black pepper to taste

50g (1/2 cup) freshly grated parmesan
   (parmigiano reggiano) cheese, plus
   extra for serving

SERVES 4-6

BREAK the head of garlic into cloves and prick each clove with a toothpick. Put the garlic cloves in a small shallow ovenproof dish and drizzle with a little olive oil. Cook in an oven preheated to 200°C (fanbake) for 15–20 minutes, or until tender and lightly browned.

Meanwhile, peel the pumpkin, remove the seeds and cut the pumpkin into small cubes (should yield 3 cups cubed pumpkin). Put the pumpkin in a medium-sized frying pan with a large knob of the butter and the rosemary. Cook for about 15 minutes over a medium heat until tender (turn often and don't let it get squishy). Turn off the heat. Peel off the papery skin from the garlic and add the whole garlic cloves to the pan of pumpkin.

Bring the chicken stock to simmering point, then set the heat so that it is kept very hot, but does not boil and evaporate.

Choose a 2.5–3 litre heavy-based saucepan or wider gratin pan. Set it over a medium heat, put in 2 tablespoons of olive oil and half of the remaining butter, and add the onion. Sauté until a pale golden colour, then pour in the wine and cook until it has nearly evaporated.

Tip in the unwashed rice, sauté for 2 minutes, stirring often with a wooden spoon, then stir in a ladleful of hot stock. This will evaporate quickly. Add a second ladleful of stock and stir gently but continuously until the stock has evaporated.

Continue cooking in this way, stirring every few seconds (if you don't stir, the rice will stick to the pan), adding more stock once the rice is no longer sloppy. The rice is ready when, like pasta, the grains are 'al dente' (still firm and only just cooked through, but no longer chalky inside).

Remove the pan from the heat, add salt, black pepper, the rest of the butter and the parmesan cheese. Beat well for 1 minute, then stir in most of the pumpkin, and the garlic, cover with a lid and leave for another minute to let the flavours fuse. Dish onto hot plates, garnish with the remaining pumpkin and serve immediately.

Titbits

This is a fairly gutsy risotto, which is perfect as a main course dish in cooler months. You'll be disappointed if you use old end-of-season garlic – it'll be too strong and acrid.

Pick up

Like all authentic risottos, this dish is dependent on the ingredients used – in this case, very fresh butter, parmigiano reggiano, proper stock and decent wine, along with fresh garlic and firm pumpkin.

Essential

Italian risotto rice. If you use anything else, it won't be risotto!
Choose a firm pumpkin, not a watery type.

Alongside

Maybe a slice or two of salami to nibble on with a glass of pinot noir while you're cooking, and a salad to follow. Nothing else.

Up front

The garlic and pumpkin can both be cooked several hours before required, the cheese can be grated a little while ahead, and, if you want to, the onion can be browned, then left in the saucepan with the heat turned off until you're ready to start cooking the risotto.

X-Factor

The health benefits and 'cure-all' claims about garlic are substantial. It is reputedly good for the intestines, can lower high blood pressure and a heavy dose of it can clear up a bad case of pimples (pity about the breath). It is widely believed to build up resistance to infection and, contrary to what many people say ('garlic repeats on me'), garlic aids digestion.

The most enduring claim is that of its antiseptic properties. It is the sulphur compounds that does the trick. As recently as World War I, the raw juice was used extensively on wounds to prevent them turning septic.

The Ultimate Hot Potato Salad

1kg starchy potatoes, peeled and cut into
   chunks
salt
butter
200g piece of bacon, cubed, or use 6
   rashers bacon, trimmed and diced
150ml cream, heated
2 cloves garlic, crushed
2 tablespoons chopped flat-leafed parsley
freshly ground black pepper to taste

SERVES 4, OR 2 SERIOUS POTATO
ADDICTS

PUT the potatoes in a saucepan, cover with cold water, add salt and bring to the boil. Cook until tender.

Meanwhile, heat a small frying pan, add a knob of butter and when it sizzles add the bacon. Cook until crisp and set aside (and try not to pick at it!).

When the potatoes are cooked, drain them, and put them in a deepish bowl, which should be heated. Then have some fun! Squish and squash them with a fork, pouring on the hot cream and adding crushed garlic and the parsley, $1/2$ teaspoon of salt and some black pepper. Scoop the bacon out of the pan with a slotted spoon and spoon on top of the mash. There's nothing left to do but to dig in!

Titbits

The name of this hot potato salad means there's nothing better, richer or more luxurious than this – it's the ultimate potato salad!

Pick up

Starchy potatoes. These are good for mashing – agria, for example, or mid- to late-season desiree.

Essential

Rich thick cream, proper bacon that's neither too salty nor too smoky, flat-leafed parsley and fresh garlic without any green sprouts.

Alongside

Try to keep a little bit of decency and serve it with a well-dressed salad of green leaves.

Up front

This is not a dinner-party dish. This is serious comfort food that you can eat late at night in private at the sink with your slippers on if that's what you feel like.

X-Factor

This is known as the thigh-padder! If you've already got love-handles, you'd better skip it.

Grilled Thyme-scented Mushrooms

MIX the first measure of olive oil, garlic, thyme sprigs, ³/₄ teaspoon of salt and black pepper to taste in a small bowl. Brush the mixture over the mushrooms, then put them, stem down, in a grill tray. Cook under a very hot grill until lightly browned, then turn and cook the other side until tender.

Alternatively, cook the mushrooms on a hot barbecue plate, cap down, for 2–3 minutes, then turn and cook briefly on the other side until tender.

While the mushrooms are cooking, prepare the salad garnish. Mix the strawberry vinegar, mustard, a few pinches of salt and black pepper to taste in a bowl. Whisk in the second measure of oil. Add the salad leaves and toss well.

Arrange the salad and hot mushrooms on plates and serve immediately.

4 tablespoons extra virgin olive oil

2 large cloves garlic, crushed

several sprigs fresh thyme, torn into small pieces

salt

freshly ground black pepper

6 large flat portabello mushrooms, trimmed

scant tablespoon strawberry vinegar

¹/₄ teaspoon Dijon mustard

2 tablespoons extra virgin olive oil

a few handfuls of assorted salad leaves (red or green lettuce, cos, lamb's lettuce, baby beetroot leaves, baby rocket, buttercrunch)

SERVES 6

Titbits

These jumbo mushrooms, scented with the tantalising aromas of fresh thyme and garlic, get a meal off to a good start.

Pick up

Slim caps of mushrooms, not the fat meaty ones. If strawberry vinegar is not available, use red wine vinegar.

Alongside

Garlic bread made with a baguette and garlic butter, or with a ciabatta and extra virgin olive oil and garlic, is a great accompaniment to these mushrooms. The wine choice has to be pinot noir – it'll love the 'woodsyness' of the mushrooms, the hint of fruity vinegar, the baby beetroot leaves in the salad, and the pungency of garlic bread.

Up front

The ingredients can be prepared ahead, but don't drizzle the mushrooms with oil until ready to cook them.

X-Factor

Mushrooms get the health tick because they offer some specific and beneficial elements to the diet. Often classed as a vegetable, they are in fact edible funghi. Garlic and salad greens, along with olive oil, turn this into a valuable dish.

Mushroom Crostini with Mustard and Thyme

50g soft butter

1 large clove garlic, crushed

¼ teaspoon Dijon mustard

1 French baguette (long French loaf)

2 tablespoons olive oil

12 medium portabello mushrooms
(don't choose the really thick caps)

sea salt to taste

freshly ground black pepper to taste

1 tablespoon chopped thyme

SERVES 4-6

BLEND the butter, garlic and mustard together in a small bowl. Slice the bread 1.5cm thick, slightly on the diagonal (you'll need 12 slices, but you may as well carrying on making them until the butter runs out, and serve the extras separately). Spread the seasoned butter on the slices of bread on one side only. Put the bread slices on a baking sheet and bake in an oven preheated to 200°C (fanbake) for 5 minutes, or until golden brown.

Once you put the bread in the oven, heat a large frying pan over a medium heat. When it is hottish, add the oil and heat until hottish. Put in the mushrooms, stalk up, and cook for about 5 minutes, seasoning them with sea salt and black pepper, or until the juices start to run. Turn them over and cook for a few minutes more, shaking the pan. Turn them stalk up again and sprinkle them with thyme, then turn off the heat.

Let the mushrooms cool for a minute, then put one on each of the bread slices. Serve on small plates – they should be eaten as soon as possible, while the bread is crisp and the mushrooms hot and juicy.

Titbits

This is really just a glorified version of mushrooms on toast and just shows that sometimes the very simple things in life can be the best. The beauty of it lies in the contrast between incredibly juicy mushrooms (consider yourself warned – you may dribble!) and crisp garlic toasts.

Pick up

Fresh, firm 'open cap' mushrooms, 8–9cm diameter. Don't buy really dense, meaty mushrooms for this recipe, as they take too long to cook all the way through. Portabello is sometimes spelled as portabella.

Alongside

You could serve these as a substantial nibble with drinks (2 per person, so this would serve 6), or as a starter with a little side salad (to serve 4–6, depending on how substantial the main course is). In both cases, a delicious pinot noir will make a great match.

Up front

It may seem too 'last minute' to cook the mushrooms, but it's actually very quick to do. The bread can be buttered the day ahead if need be. Put the slices in a plastic container, separating each layer with waxed paper.

X-Factor

Mushrooms contain a healthy mix of iron, zinc, potassium and B group vitamins.

Mushroom, Leek and Potato Soup

4 medium leeks

50g butter

2 sticks celery, sliced

2 medium carrots, sliced

4 medium potatoes (about 700g), peeled and thinly sliced

250g Swiss brown mushrooms (brown buttons), quartered

250g large portabello mushrooms (choose big thick caps), thickly sliced

2 fresh bay leaves

1 $\frac{3}{4}$ teaspoons salt

1.5 litres water

chopped flat-leafed parsley or snipped chives to garnish

SERVES AT LEAST 8

USE a large knife to cut off the tops of the leeks, then shave off any tough parts and remove any coarse outer leaves. Trim off the roots, cut each leek in two lengthways, then rinse thoroughly under running water. Slice thinly.

Melt the butter in a large saucepan, then add the leeks, celery and carrots. Toss them in the butter over heat for 3–5 minutes, then lay the potatoes on top. Don't stir the potatoes through the leeks, because if they sit on the bottom of the saucepan they can catch. Cover the pan and cook on a very gentle heat for 20 minutes.

Add both types of mushrooms and the bay leaves, stir the salt through and add the water. Bring the soup just to boiling point, stirring often, then immediately turn the heat to low. Partially cover with a lid and cook very gently for 20 minutes, or until the vegetables are tender.

Remove the bay leaves and purée the soup in batches, in a food processor or liquidiser, and return to the cleaned pan.

Reheat gently, check for seasoning, then ladle into bowls and garnish with a little chopped parsley or snipped chives.

Titbits

This is a tasty, bulky soup full of goodness – just the thing for a wintry Sunday lunch with a loaf of crusty bread. I like the soup chunky, and purée about half of it, leaving the rest in chunks – the perfect texture.

Pick up

Fresh, sweet-tasting leeks, not withered ones which are stringy and strong to eat. Mid-season potatoes are perfect for this; you don't want them to dissolve totally in the soup, but nor do you want very firm slices that won't break up, because some of the potatoes' starch is needed to thicken the soup. Choose big brown, meaty mushrooms, rather than pale button ones, because they have more flavour and colour.

Essential

The salt. Cut it back and the soup will taste like dishwater!

Alongside

As mentioned, bread is all that you need to turn this into a comforting supper or light meal.

Up-front

Like most soups, this can be made ahead and reheated.

X-Factor

Leeks contain antioxidants and are good for the blood, containing plenty of vitamin A, some B group vitamins, and iron, potassium, calcium and fibre. Mix them in a saucepan with celery, carrots, potatoes and mushrooms, and you've got a life-giving brew.

Ever wondered why celery often tastes bitter? More sprays are used on celery than on many other vegetables. With celery you eat the lot, including the bits that got sprayed, because there's no skin to peel off as there is on, say, pumpkin. Therefore wash celery extremely well, scrubbing it gently with a vegetable brush. The answer really, of course, is to buy organic. Celery's biggest claim to fame is its fibre content, but it also has plenty of potassium and calcium.

Spicy Red Lentil Dhal

WASH the lentils thoroughly in a sieve under cold running water until the water runs clear.

Grind the coriander and cumin seeds. Heat the olive oil or ghee in a large saucepan over a low to medium heat. Add the onions and fry until golden. Add the garlic, chilli powder, ginger, turmeric, and the ground coriander and cumin. Fry for 1 minute, then add the drained lentils. Turn them with a spoon so they are coated with the spicy mixture, then add the water.

Bring to the boil, turn the heat to low and cover with a lid. Cook gently for 40–50 minutes, or until the mixture is porridge-like. Stir often during the last minutes of cooking to prevent the dhal catching on the bottom of the pan. Stir in the salt and lemon juice, then let the dhal cool before serving.

250g (1¼ cups) red lentils
1½ teaspoons coriander seeds
1½ teaspoons cumin seeds
3 tablespoons olive oil or ghee
2 onions, sliced
2 cloves garlic, chopped
1 teaspoon chilli powder (ground dried chillies)
½ teaspoon ground ginger
½ teaspoon ground turmeric
750ml hot water
¼ teaspoon salt
1 tablespoon lemon juice

SERVES 4-6

Titbits

Pulses are the edible seeds of leguminous plants, which include peas, beans and lentils. Lentils are round and flattish in shape and vary in size and colour, and they can be sold whole or skinned and split. They have been cultivated since prehistoric times. Dhal (or dal) is the generic Indian name used for dried lentils, peas and beans, and also the name of any dish that features them as a major ingredient.

Dhal, the dish, can be made thin and soupy, plain ploppy or scoop-upable! But it is always delicious when well made. This dhal, made from inexpensive and readily available red lentils, has plenty of punch and it can be finished off in various ways. Try it with a big swirl of plain yoghurt on top and a handful of chopped coriander. Chopped fresh red chillies can also be added to give a biting heat.

Alternatively, heat a little oil or ghee and lightly fry a few strips of lemon peel, a dozen peppercorns, a few crushed cardamom seeds, and a pinch each of fennel and coriander seeds for a few minutes until fragrant. You can add a little crushed dried chilli if you want. Pour this over the warm dhal and serve.

Essential

Fresh spices. To get the most out of spices, buy them whole and grind them as required.

Alongside

This is best eaten warmish. Serve with Indian breads, steamed rice and other spicy vegetable dishes, with plenty of yoghurt, to make a balanced vegetarian meal.

Up front

Dhal can be made up to 48 hours ahead; keep it covered and refrigerated. This is particularly helpful when making an Indian feast.

X-Factor

Don't hold back when the dhal is passed around; lentils are an excellent source of protein, making them hugely important in the vegetarian Indian diet – and they also contain iron, calcium, potassium and B group vitamins. Remember that the protein from plants is incomplete (unlike meat which has complete protein), but around 30% more of the protein plants contain is made available to the body if the lentils are eaten with cereal (in this case, Indian breads).

Low-fat yoghurt provides calcium and protein and, if you choose a yoghurt containing acidophilus culture, you'll keep your gut healthy, too. The dhal also contains onions and garlic, so give yourself a real boost and make enough for leftovers!

Moroccan Lentil Soup with Silverbeet

WASH the lentils thoroughly in a sieve under cold running water until the water runs clear.

Put the onion and garlic in a large saucepan with the olive oil. Cover with a lid and cook gently for about 10 minutes, until just starting to brown. Crush the cumin and coriander seeds in a mortar with a pestle, or crush with a rolling pin between two sheets of kitchen paper. Add to the onion and garlic, cook for 1 minute, then stir in the tomatoes, black pepper and lentils. Add the water and bring to the boil.

Lower the heat and cook gently, uncovered, for about 30 minutes, or until the lentils are tender.

Plunge the silverbeet into a saucepan of lightly salted, gently boiling water and cook for 5 minutes. Drain. If using spinach, it is not necessary to blanch it.

When the lentils are tender, cool the soup for 10 minutes. Strain it through a sieve and blend the lentils until smooth in a food processor or liquidiser with enough of the liquid to make the mixture flow (keep the rest of the liquid to thin the soup if necessary). Return to the cleaned saucepan and season with 1 teaspoon of salt (or to taste), add the blanched silverbeet or chopped spinach and enough soup liquid to bring it to the right consistency. Cook for 10 minutes more, or until the silverbeet is tender. Serve the soup with bowls of chopped coriander, harissa, yoghurt and lemon wedges.

250g (1$\frac{1}{3}$ cups) brown lentils, rinsed
1 large onion, thinly sliced
2 cloves garlic, finely chopped
4 tablespoons extra virgin olive oil
1 teaspoon cumin seeds
1 teaspoon coriander seeds
4 medium vine-ripened tomatoes, coarsely chopped
freshly ground black pepper to taste
2 litres water
salt
350g young silverbeet (Swiss chard) or spinach leaves, trimmed, washed and finely chopped
chopped coriander
harissa
plain yoghurt
1 lemon, cut into wedges

SERVES 4

Titbits

This soup, with its melded spicy flavours, breathtaking bite of harissa cooled with dollops of yoghurt, and the fresh acid sweep of lemon, is memorable, head-clearing, rib-sticking stuff.

Pick up

Fresh young silverbeet or spinach leaves. I used organically grown multi-hued silverbeet in the recipe photographed.
Harissa is an oily, fiery-hot North African chilli paste, brick red to bright orangy red in colour.

Essential

The yoghurt, harissa, lemon and coriander – it turns brown sludge into a knockout soup.

Alongside

Warmed puffy pita breads.

Up front

The soup happily sits in the fridge for 24 hours or so, but it is best if you add the silverbeet when you reheat it.

X-Factor

Lentils are a valuable and inexpensive source of protein and contain good amounts of iron, calcium, potassium and the B vitamins thiamine and nicotinic acid. They are low in fat, high in dietary fibre and carbohydrates and are easily digested. Vitamin C is produced if the lentils are sprouted. (Sprout them only until the growth is the same length of the seed.)
Lentils and beans are an excellent source of protein, but the protein is incomplete (unlike meat which has complete protein). However, around 30% more of the protein is made available to the body if the lentils are eaten with cereal. Some of the oldest dishes in the world are based on this knowledge (for example – Indian dhals with rice or with Indian breads, Middle Eastern dishes of chick peas and grains, even baked beans on toast). Serving this soup with pita breads brings it into this category.
Silverbeet is also very high in antioxidants.

Pear and Parmesan Salad

4 firmish pears
juice of 1–2 lemons
2 baby cos lettuces
3 tablespoons extra virgin olive oil
sea salt
freshly ground black pepper to taste
small block parmesan (parmigiano
    reggiano) cheese

SERVES 4-6

WASH and dry the pears and slice into thinnish slivers. Put the pears in a large bowl and gently toss 2 tablespoons of lemon juice through them, making sure that all cut surfaces are coated. Break the cos lettuces into leaves, wash and dry them and put them in a large salad bowl. Put the pears on top. Drizzle with the oil, sprinkle with a little sea salt and grind on some black pepper. Toss gently. Use a small vegetable peeler to peel off slivers of parmesan and let them fall into the salad. Serve immediately.

Titbits

How can something so simple be so sublime? Only by having premium ingredients – this is not the place for cost-cutting.

Pick up

An exquisite estate-bottled extra virgin olive oil – it'll add so much to the salad. If cos lettuce is not available, substitute buttercrunch, or some other mild-tasting lettuce.

Essential

Fragrant pears are a must-have. Give them the sniff test before buying (they should be sweetly perfumed).

Alongside

This is a light starter perfect for autumn or winter. Follow it with lighter meats such as chicken, or pork, or seafood. If you can find a pinot gris with a hint of pear fragrance and gentle fruitiness, you'll have a superb match.

Up front

The salad should be made just prior to serving but the cos lettuce could be washed, dried and kept refrigerated in a plastic bag.

X-Factor

Pears contain antioxidants and using them in savoury dishes helps get more of them in the diet. Cos lettuce contributes nutrients, and the lemon winds up the vitamin C content. Parmigiano reggiano (Italian parmesan cheese) is a nutrient-dense food. You can feel good about having seconds of this salad.

Pea and Ham Soup

BROTH: Rinse the ham bones and put them in a large deep saucepan with the vegetables and seasonings. Pour the cold water in. Bring to the boil, then skim off any foam, partially cover with a lid and cook gently for 4 hours. Strain. When the bones are cool enough to handle, pick over and set aside any appetising pieces of meat, chop them coarsely, put them in a container, cool, cover and refrigerate.

Cool the broth, then cover it and keep it refrigerated until the next day. When ready to carry on with the recipe, remove the broth from the fridge and spoon off any congealed fat.

SOUP: Put the onion, garlic and butter in a very large saucepan with 1 tablespoon of water. Cover with a lid and cook gently for 5–7 minutes until softened. Stir the peas in, then pour in the ham broth; if necessary, make up the quantity to 4 litres with water.

Bring to the boil, skim, then lower the heat and partially cover with a lid. Cook gently for about 1½ hours, or until the peas are very tender. Add the chopped ham meat, check the seasoning, adding salt if required, and black pepper. Cook for 15 minutes more, then ladle into bowls. Sprinkle with parsley and serve.

Titbits

First, you need a ham bone. If you've cooked a ham in warm weather, the last thing you'll feel like doing with the leftover bone is making a wintry soup. Save the bone. Wrap it and store it in the freezer until one day in the middle of winter, when you can't shake the cold out of your bones, and you yearn for the comforts of a good old-fashioned soup, you'll be thankful that you didn't give the bone to the dog!

What you also need to do is to save some of the meat along with the bone. Cut off all the tiddly bits, fat and gristle included, then sort it into piles – the less appetising bits for the broth, the good bits for the soup, and wrap and label everything, then put it in the freezer with the bone. Roll on winter!

If you can, start the soup a day before you want to serve it, so that the broth can cool. The fat then comes to the surface and can be removed easily.

The broth can be frozen at this point if you wish to make the soup at a later date (you could freeze it as soon as it is cool enough, before chilling it and skimming the fat, if you need to, then thaw and skim the fat before using it). There are so many options!

Pick up

A ham, of course. Look for one that is not too salty or smoky. How can you tell? You can't, apart from using your nose and gauging the smokiness or cure that's been used. Failing a leftover ham bone, you could buy bones from the butcher and fresh sliced ham off the bone. This is the expensive way of doing it, but sometimes when you're desperate...

Alongside

Crusty bread, nothing more. It's a meal in itself.

Up front

You can make the broth a day ahead, or months ahead and freeze it. You can make the soup the day you want to serve it, or up to 48 hours in advance, or freeze it. It's very flexible.

X-Factor

It smells like Mum's home cooking. Sometimes you need that. Of course you're getting the benefit of all the vegetables too. Think of it as an army of soldiers (antioxidants) that are on the warpath to kill off any intruders (free radicals) – one cup is like a cure-all!

Broth

bones of a cooked ham (ham on the bone), around 1.2–1.5kg
1 large onion, quartered
1 stick celery, cut into chunks
1 large carrot, cut into chunks
1 tablespoon chopped thyme
12 peppercorns
2 bay leaves
4.5 litres cold water

Soup

1 large onion, finely chopped
2 large cloves garlic, crushed
1 tablespoon butter
1 tablespoon water, plus more if needed
675g (3 cups) split green peas, well rinsed under running water in a sieve
4 litres ham broth
225–300g (1½–2 cups) ham chunks, taken off the bone, chopped (do not include fat or gristle; this can go in the broth)
salt to taste (you probably won't need any because of the salt in the ham)
freshly ground black pepper to taste
2 tablespoons chopped flat-leafed parsley

SERVES 8–10

Butterflies with Tomato and Green Pea Sauce

1 medium onion, chopped (not too finely)

2 rashers bacon, rind removed, finely chopped

4 tablespoons extra virgin olive oil

250g frozen baby peas

1 large clove garlic, crushed

60ml (1/4 cup) dry white wine

600g canned Italian tomatoes, mashed

1 teaspoon chopped fresh marjoram

salt to taste

freshly ground black pepper to taste

500g farfalle pasta (butterflies)

freshly grated parmesan (parmigiano reggiano) cheese for serving

SERVES 4–6 (4 AS A MAIN OR 6 AS A STARTER)

PUT the onion and bacon in a saucepan with the olive oil and cook gently and slowly until lightly browned. Put the peas in a sieve and rinse under hot running water to wash off any ice crystals. Add the garlic to the pan, stir, then add the peas. Splash with white wine, cook briefly to evaporate, then add the tomatoes and the marjoram. Season with salt and black pepper.

Cook gently for 30 minutes, partially covered with a lid. If the sauce is too liquid, continue cooking without the lid for 5–10 minutes more.

Cook the pasta in plenty of gently boiling, well-salted water until al dente. Drain and tip into a heated serving bowl. Pour the sauce over, toss well and serve immediately with parmesan cheese.

Titbits

An easy pasta dish which appeals to all palates. Serve the sauce on pennette, mezze penne or dried gnocchi, as well as farfalle.

Pick up

Frozen baby peas. My Italian sister-in-law Marcella, who would serve this as a first course for lunch, followed by a main course of meat and salad, always uses frozen peas in the sauce; she reserves fresh peas for dishes where they can be the star of the show. I totally agree with her.

Essential

Italian canned tomatoes – the fleshy tomatoes smell of the sun.

Alongside

This is a standard Biuso recipe which I make for a quick mid-week family dinner, accompanied by a salad. An inexpensive chianti is the usual tipple with this pasta.

Up front

The sauce can be made a day in advance if need be; reheat gently when required.

X-Factor

Peas, pasta, parmigiano, pomodori (tomatoes) – all great stuff.

Fresh and frozen peas should have plenty of vitamin C, but it just may be that frozen peas have more than fresh, if they were processed immediately after picking, and the fresh ones hang around a few days in the shops. Peas have a healthy mix of vitamins and minerals, including B group vitamins, vitamins A and K, folate and potassium, and fibre.

Split Green Pea and Bacon Soup

500g potatoes, peeled and cut into large
  chunks
225g (1 cup) split green peas, well rinsed
  under running water in a sieve
2 litres light stock
1 tablespoon olive oil
2 knobs butter
100g middle bacon, derinded and finely
  chopped
1 large onion, finely chopped
1 large clove garlic, crushed
6 fresh sage leaves, chopped
2 tablespoons coarsely chopped flat-leafed
  parsley
1 teaspoon salt
freshly ground black pepper to taste
freshly grated parmesan (parmigiano
  reggiano) cheese for serving

SERVES 4-6

PUT the potatoes, split peas and stock in a saucepan. Bring to the boil and skim off any froth, then lower the heat, partially cover with a lid and cook gently for about an hour, or until the peas are tender; don't worry if the potatoes fall apart.

Meanwhile, put the oil and butter in a large frying pan. Add the bacon and cook for about 7 minutes over a medium heat. Add the onion, garlic and sage and cook, stirring occasionally, until golden brown. Set aside.

Put the parsley in the bowl of a food processor, or in a liquidiser, and add 2–3 ladlefuls of soup. Blend until the parsley is chopped and the liquid has turned green. Add more of the soup and blend until smooth. Transfer to a bowl and add the rest of the soup. Wash and dry the saucepan and pour the soup back in.

Add the salt, a few grinds of black pepper and the onion mixture (scrape in all the butter and oil). Set back over a medium heat and bring to the boil, stirring gently. Lower the heat, partially cover with a lid and cook gently for another 5 minutes. Serve with the parmesan cheese.

Titbits

Usually, green pea soup is a dull colour, but this one is given a pretty, green hue by blending parsley in a food processor to extract its strong green colour before adding it to the soup. The addition of bacon, garlic, onion and sage is quite remarkable, providing a background spicy sweet flavour – you might like to keep some of the bacon and onion mixture to put in the centre of each bowl of soup.

Pick up

All-purpose starchy potatoes because they thicken the soup.

Essential

Fresh sage – don't use dried sage because it is excessively strong and has lost its warm spicy notes.

Alongside

Like all big pots of goodness, this just needs a loaf of decent bread and good company to satisfy the soul. A little red wine to follow always helps, of course!

Corn and Bacon Chowder

PLUNGE the corn cobs into a pot of boiling water, partially cover with a lid, bring the water back to the boil and cook for 10 minutes. Scoop the corn cobs out of the water and cool on a chopping board. Reduce the corn cooking water over a high heat for 15 minutes.

Put the bacon in a medium-sized saucepan with the onion, garlic, celery and butter. Cover with a lid and cook very gently for 10 minutes, or until everything is tender.

As soon as the cobs are cool enough to handle, scrape off the kernels with a sharp knife.

Add the potatoes to the bacon mixture, along with the milk and measured corn cooking water (keep the rest of the corn water to thin the soup if necessary). Season with salt and pepper and bring to the boil. Cook gently for 15 minutes, partially covered with a lid, then add the corn kernels. Mash the soup with a potato masher, squashing the potato into a purée so that it thickens the soup, and crushing some of the corn to release flavour and colour.

Cook for 15 minutes more, mashing with the potato masher from time to time, and stirring the soup so that it doesn't catch on the bottom of the pan. The soup should be wonderfully thick and chunky; thin it with a little more corn water if necessary.

Check the soup for seasoning, stir the parsley or coriander through, then dish into soup bowls.

1.2kg frozen corn

4 rashers bacon, derinded and finely chopped

1 onion, finely chopped

2 cloves garlic, crushed

2 sticks celery, chopped

1 tablespoon butter

350g (2 medium) starchy potatoes, peeled and diced

750ml (3 cups) milk

375ml (1½ cups) cooking water from boiling the corn

1 teaspoon salt, or to taste

freshly ground black pepper to taste

2 tablespoons chopped parsley or coriander

SERVES 4 AS A SOUP MEAL WITH BREAD, OR 6 AS A STARTER

Titbits

This wonderfully thick and chunky soup is a real toe-warmer. It's the kind of thing to whip up on a chilly day when your body needs warming, nourishing food.

Pick-up

Frozen corn cobs are better than canned or frozen corn kernels because they have more corn flavour, and you can boil the cobs to extract even more corn flavour.

Alongside

Garlic bread may not be the 'in' thing, but it works a treat with this soup. Otherwise, opt for a crusty loaf.

Up front

The soup keeps well for a day, so you can make it well in advance.

X-Factor

All the goodies from onion, garlic, celery, corn and herbs, with calcium from milk, make this a nutritious brew.

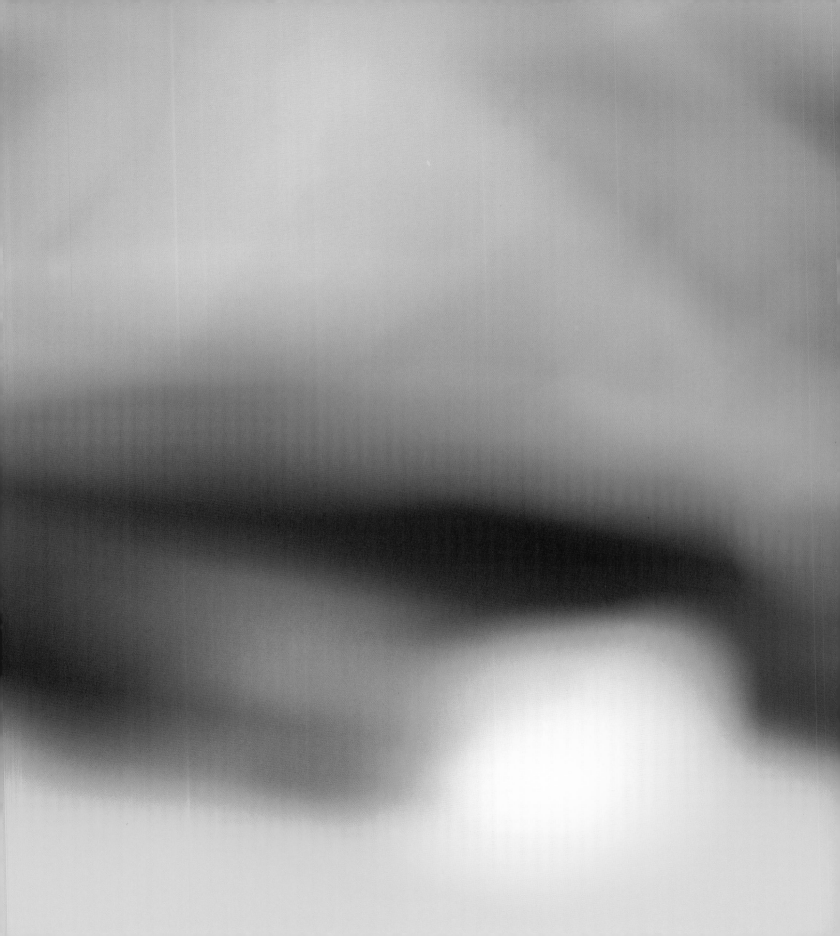

home comforts

Lamb in a Pot

salt

freshly ground black pepper to taste

4 cloves garlic, crushed

3 rashers bacon, finely diced

1 tablespoon finely chopped thyme

1 tablespoon finely chopped marjoram

1 boned forequarter of lamb, trimmed, around 1kg after boning (if the joint has been tied, untie it, trim excess fat away, put on the seasoning and tie up again)

1 tablespoon olive oil

125ml (1/2 cup) beer

1kg potatoes, peeled and cut into chunks

1 large onion, peeled and cut into thick strips through the root end

2 carrots, peeled and cut into thick chunks

2 sticks celery, cut into thick sticks

SERVES 4-6

MIX 1/2 teaspoon of salt, plenty of pepper, the garlic, bacon, thyme and marjoram in a small bowl. Spread the seasoning over the inside of the lamb, then roll it into shape and tie with string. Heat the olive oil in a heavy-based casserole and when hot add the joint of meat and brown well on all sides, turning with tongs.

Pour the beer over and quickly surround the meat with potatoes, then add the onion, carrots and celery. Sprinkle a teaspoon of salt over and cover with a tight-fitting lid. Turn the element down to a low setting and cook for about 1 1/2 hours, or until the vegetables and meat are very tender.

Transfer the meat to a board and the vegetables to a heated serving plate; cover the vegetables loosely with aluminium foil. If the juices in the casserole are on the thin side, thicken them with a little cornflour mixed with water. Put the casserole over a medium heat and stir until boiling. Season with salt and black pepper. If there's not much juice, add a little stock and thicken if required.

Slice the meat thinly and arrange on a heated plate, spoon the juices over and serve immediately with the vegetables.

Titbits

This is a great family dish. Everyone will start sniffing the air while it's cooking, begging you for dinner. I reckon it's the never-fail combination of celery, carrot and onion with the bacon and beer which does it. Brown the meat slowly to develop good colour and flavour. If the vegetables don't brown, finish them off in a non-stick frying pan in a knob of sizzling butter.

It's the acidity in beer which helps to tenderise meats, making it a good addition to casseroles or stews made with the cheaper cuts of meat such as the forequarter of lamb used here. It also works a treat with rabbit, pheasant and quail – even chicken can benefit. But it does more than just tenderise meat. Imagine a lamb stew made with herbs, tomato, garlic and onion, with the flavours sitting one on top of the other, not amalgamated. The lamb flavour, which develops a hint of savoury caramel flavour during browning in hot oil, is at the bottom,

with a layer of sweet onion on top. Next, a hint of pungency from crushed garlic, then some aromatic nuances from herbs come in and a refreshing acidic swipe from tomato at the end. Adding beer to the brew pulls all the flavours together as they cook, underpinning the dish with a spicy sweetness, or smoky nuttiness, depending on the chosen beer.

Pick up

A beer which is not too bitter, nor too sweet. Otherwise there are no rules. The hoppy, yeasty, fruity, smoky, caramelly, toasty, spicy, oaky and nutty characters found in beers all add their individual characters to the dish. Other suitable cuts of meat are boned leg of lamb and boned shoulder of lamb. I have made this dish successfully with new potatoes, which keep their shape, and with mid-season starchy potatoes, which collapse a bit and thicken the juices – both are good.

Alongside

A green vegetable such as leek is all that's required. I'd go for a fruity, spicy beer as a liquid refreshment.

Up front

The lamb can be stuffed and tied in shape up to a day ahead, but it should be served immediately after cooking.

X-Factor

This is a wholesome meat dish with plenty of goodness from garlic, vegetables and beer.

Pot-roasted Fresh Silverside

1.5kg piece fresh silverside

2 tablespoons olive oil

2 large onions, quartered

2 large carrots, quartered

1 large parsnip, quartered

3 sticks celery, cut in chunks

1¼ teaspoons salt

freshly ground black pepper to taste

1 tablespoon finely chopped thyme or
   lemon thyme

3 fresh bay leaves

1 tablespoon soft butter blended with 2
   teaspoons plain flour (for thickening)

SERVES 8

RINSE and pat the meat dry with absorbent kitchen paper, then tie it with string to help keep it in shape during cooking. Heat the olive oil in a heavy casserole (I use a cast iron casserole with a 6-litre capacity) and brown the meat on both sides, turning with tongs. Transfer the meat to a side plate and add the onions, carrots, parsnip and celery to the casserole. Brown evenly, over a fairly high heat.

Season the meat on all sides with the salt and return it to the casserole. Grind on some pepper and add the thyme and bay leaves. Cover with a tight-fitting lid and pot roast (cook over an element) over a very low heat for 1½–2 hours, or until the meat is very tender. If preferred, the casserole can be placed in an oven preheated to 170°C (regular) and cooked for 1½ hours.

Transfer the meat to a chopping board and the vegetables to a heated plate to keep warm. Skim any fat from the juices in the casserole, then bring the juices to the boil (you'll be surprised how much juice the meat and vegetables give out). Whisk in the blended butter and flour, bubble for a minute, then check for seasoning. Carve the meat and place on a heated platter with the vegetables. Spoon a little gravy over and serve the rest in a heated jug.

Titbits

Pot roasting involves browning meat in an ovenproof casserole or pot, sometimes adding stock or wine, along with vegetables, covering with a lid, then cooking slowly on the stove top or in the oven. Cutting the onions through the root end helps hold them together.

Pick up

Silverside is usually sold corned, so you will need to order it a few days in advance from a butcher, but it is well worth it. You could try it with corned silverside, or with rolled brisket, or even a leg or shoulder of lamb.

Essential

Browning the meat and vegetables until they develop a good rich colour, and cooking them slowly in their own juices gives the hearty flavour in this dish. If you take a shortcut, it'll show!

Alongside

Crunchy jacket-baked potatoes are my favourite with this dish (use starchy potatoes, scrub the skin clean, rub with salt and bake for 1½ hours in an oven preheated to 200°C (fanbake), or until the interior is soft and the skin crunchy). Cabernet sauvignon will be a happy match with this meal.

Up front

It takes no more than 10 minutes to prepare, and it is all done well ahead of serving time.

X-Factor

This dish captures all the goodness of slowly cooked meat and vegetables – plenty of B vitamins from beef, along with zinc and iron, and a comprehensive range of vitamins and minerals from the vegetables.
It's easy to forget the power of slow-cooked meat and vegetables with their flavoursome juices trapped under a lid, slices of tender and tasty meat napped with its own barely thickened juice, clear and glossy and aromatic.

The Big Steak

CUT the meat into four steaks about 5cm thick. Flatten them slightly to make them even. Spread 1½ teaspoons of the mustard around the sides of the steaks. Grind on plenty of black pepper, then put the steaks in a dish, cover, and refrigerate until required.

Heat a medium-sized, heavy-based frying pan (cast-iron is ideal) over a very high heat. Put in 1½ tablespoons of olive oil. When the oil is hot, put in the steaks. Cook for about 4 minutes a side for rare to medium-rare. Transfer to a plate and remove the pan from the heat. Season the steaks generously with salt. Let the pan cool briefly. If the pan is dry, add a little more olive oil. Add the garlic and cook gently until just starting to colour, then add the stock and bubble up until reduced by about half. Add the chopped mint and extra mustard, and season with salt. Pour a puddle of the reduced juices onto four heated dinner plates. Put the steaks on top and serve immediately.

750g piece of beef fillet cut from the thick
   end, trimmed of fat and any silvery skin
3 teaspoons Dijon mustard
freshly ground black pepper to taste
2½ tablespoons olive oil
salt
2 cloves garlic, crushed
125ml (½ cup) beef stock
2 tablespoons chopped mint

SERVES 4

Titbits

Salt the meat after cooking (unless stated) otherwise it can make the surface of the meat wet and cause spitting, and it can draw out the juices too early, especially when added to a marinade.
Invest in a splatter screen. This is a netted metal screen which you place over the top of the pan. Unlike when you use a lid, air can still circulate, so the steaks continue to fry and don't stew as they would if steam was trapped in with a lid. They keep about 70% of the splatters in the pan.
Let the steaks rest for 5 minutes before serving. This allows the meat to reabsorb its juices, making it more succulent in the mouth.

Touch test for cooked beef

* Very rare beef 'gives' under pressure, feels very soft to the touch, juices clear.
* Rare beef feels soft to the touch.
* Medium-rare beef feels soft and springy to the touch.
* Medium beef feels firm and springy to the touch, juices pink.
* Well-done beef feels firm to the touch, juices clear.
* Very-well-done beef feels very firm to the touch.

Pick up

Good quality beef. All of the tips here will help, but the best bit of advice I can give is for you to get to know your butcher. Explain to the butcher what you expect from a fresh meat supplier. I believe we all need to support our local butchers, but you may need to guide them. If you don't give them your business, like the fruiterer and fishmonger, they'll disappear down the gurgler.

Alongside

I'd go for a parsnip mash or, in mid-winter, a mash made with celeriac and potato, and serve the mash with a bowl of perky Brussels sprouts, baby bok choy or broccoli, or cabbage tossed with a little sautéed onion and crispy bacon. As for a wine, you can go all out – grab a big grunty Australian red such as a shiraz – there's nothing it will like more than a piece of red meat it can sink its tannins into.

Up front

Make sure you have the beef at room temperature before cooking; if it is stone cold it will take longer for it to cook and it will not cook evenly.

X-Factor

Beef is a powerhouse of B vitamins and has dollops of iron, zinc, phosphorous and potassium. If it is well trimmed, less than half of its fat is saturated.

Best-ever Bacon and Egg Pie

ROLL out the pastry thinly and line half of it into a shallow pie plate (23cm diameter x 4–5cm deep). Beat the whole eggs and 2 yolks with the sea salt, black pepper, cream and sage leaves. Line the pastry with one-third of the bacon rashers, then pour in one-third of the egg mixture. Make two more layers, distributing the sage leaves evenly.

Cover with pastry and use some of the egg mixture to stick the bottom and top pieces of pastry together. Crimp the edges. Make a hole in the centre of the pie for the steam to escape. Chill the pie before baking (bake it straight from the refrigerator).

Blend the remaining egg yolk with a few drops of water and a few pinches of salt. Brush over the top of the pastry. Cook in an oven preheated to 200°C (fanbake) for around 30 minutes, or until the pastry is very well browned.

350g purchased puff pastry, thawed
5 eggs, plus 3 yolks
$1/4$ teaspoon sea salt
freshly ground black pepper to taste
60ml ($1/4$ cup) cream
24 fresh sage leaves
250g streaky bacon, rind removed

SERVES 8 OR MORE

Titbits

What you decide to put in a bacon and egg pie is up to you – but I never include tomatoes, because they can make everything go soggy. My secret ingredient is cream. It keeps everything moist but not wet, and adds a richness I think the pie needs. I don't like lumps of cooked egg white, so I whisk the egg whites and yolks together with the cream. This also means there'll be no bullet-hard egg yolks. And last but not least, sage leaves. The spicy pungency of sage melding with the savoury smoky taste of bacon is just sensational. It's the best bacon and egg pie recipe ever (thanks to my friend Tessa)!

Pick up

Streaky bacon of good quality. If you buy bacon in a packet swimming in liquid, that's what you'll get – watery bacon with the flavour washed out (which, consequently, is impossible to fry well). Buy dry, thinly sliced bacon, with some fat, which will provide sweetness and moisture.

Essential

Quality puff pastry. You don't have to make it yourself (I only make it about once a decade just to check I can still do it!), but what you buy must be made properly, with butter. Avoid supermarket 'no frills' puff pastry.

Alongside

This is picnic fare – tomatoes, salad, gherkins – anything really. A bottle of gewürztraminer will work wonders with the spiciness of sage and bacon.

Up front

The ideal temperature to serve the pie, in my opinion, is while it is still warm. If you're taking it on a picnic, cook it just before leaving home. Remove from the oven and transport it in the pie dish; don't cover it. By the time you get to your picnic spot you'll be ravenous as the glorious smells of savoury bacon, spicy sage and buttery pastry fill the air!

X-Factor

Let's be reasonable – this is a high-fat dish (pastry, cream, bacon and eggs), which is okay to eat once in a while. Balance it with a salad.

Sautéed Brussels Sprout Leaves

Brussels sprouts (allow about 3 per
    person)
salt
butter
freshly ground black pepper to taste
a few grates of nutmeg

SERVES 6

TRIM the Brussels sprouts, then peel off the leaves, trimming away more from the bottom when you can no longer peel off any more leaves; the very tiny ones in the centre of each sprout will be unusable.

When all the Brussels sprouts are prepared, rinse the leaves. Plunge them into a large saucepan of boiling salted water and cook, uncovered, for 3–4 minutes, or until nearly tender. Drain and rinse well with cold water until the leaves feel cool (this helps to keep their green colour). Shake well and leave to drain.

Five minutes before serving, heat a large frying pan or wok over a low heat. Add a large knob of butter and when it is melted drop in the leaves. Stirfry until very hot but still crisp-tender. If the leaves start to catch on the bottom of the pan, add a tablespoon of stock or water (they mustn't fry or they will lose their colour).

Sprinkle with a little salt, and grind on some pepper and nutmeg. Tip into a serving dish and serve immediately (don't cover).

Titbits

Soggy sprouts are a bad childhood food memory for many. But separated into leaves, blanched and reheated in hot butter, they can attend even the most stylish dinner party. If you're trying to serve these to an anti-sprout brigade, pass them off as baby cabbage leaves!

Essential

More than any other vegetable (apart from cabbage) Brussels sprouts must be in pristine condition to be worth eating. I'm talking crisp, green, compact buds – anything else is pig fodder. Brussels sprouts are at their peak after they've had their first fright of frost.

Alongside

Serve these as a winter green vegetable in place of broccoli and cabbage.

Up front

The leaves can be blanched 2–3 hours before finishing off; keep at room temperature, uncovered.

X-Factor

Not surprisingly, these little green things are good for you. They've got plenty of vitamin C, some B vitamins and potassium, and, it's claimed, they help to prevent some cancers.

Hot Asparagus with Sizzled Ham and Potatoes

500g new potatoes, scrubbed and
 steamed
350g fat asparagus spears, woody ends
 snapped off, trimmed
salt
butter
several thickly sliced pieces of ham off the
 bone
freshly ground black pepper to taste
freshly grated parmesan (parmigiano
 reggiano) cheese for sprinkling (optional)

SERVES 4

EITHER steam or boil the potatoes. When they are half tender, plunge the asparagus into a saucepan of boiling salted water and cook gently for several minutes until done to your liking. Drain, refresh with cold water, then drain again.

Put the asparagus in a saucepan of boiling, lightly salted water, tips pointing up. Cook with the lid off for 2–5 minutes. Drain and refresh with plenty of cold water.

Heat a frying pan with a knob of butter and, when hot, add the ham. Fry briefly until golden around the edges.

Peel and slice the potatoes into rounds and arrange on four heated plates. Put the ham on top of the potatoes. Roll the asparagus around in the hot pan the ham was cooked in, seasoning with salt and black pepper, then arrange the asparagus on the ham. Top with parmesan cheese, if using, and serve immediately.

Titbits

This is a great supper dish, like a glorified dish of ham and eggs (see Alongside) with a few extras thrown in.

Asparagus is an easy vegetable to prepare, requiring nothing more than a snap or a trim to remove any woody ends and a quick wash. Plunging it into boiling water sets the colour. Cooking with the lid off lets vegetable acids escape in the steam; putting a lid on makes the acids fall back onto the asparagus, which can discolour it.

Pick up

New potatoes, fresh asparagus, juicy ham. Although this is the sort of thing you might whip up with the remnants to be found in the fridge just before you go shopping again, withered asparagus, greening potatoes and dried ham will just not cut the mustard.

Alongside

If you want to make this more substantial, top each plate with a fried or poached egg. I think it needs a loaf of ciabatta, or something similar, heated in the oven until the centre is soft and warm and the crust crunchy. Serve a glass of gewürztraminer or sauvignon blanc with this dish.

Up front

This is one of those dishes that you make and eat immediately.

X-Factor

Asparagus is a valuable vegetable to include in the diet. It contains a generous collection of vitamins from the A, B and C groups, along with plenty of potassium, good amounts of calcium, magnesium and phosphorous. It also has good quantities of folic acid and rutin (an antioxidant). It has practically no fat, contains some fibre and is low in calories.

Apple and Rhubarb Crumble

SIFT the flour into a bowl and add the butter. Rub in with your fingertips or use a pastry blender until well amalgamated, then mix in 3 tablespoons of the brown sugar, the almonds and lemon zest.

Lightly butter a 20cm round shallow baking dish. Peel the apples, discard cores and slice thinly. Mix in the dish with the prepared rhubarb and the rest of the brown sugar. (If the apples are very tart, add another tablespoon of sugar.)

Spoon the crumble topping over the fruit, ensuring all the fruit is covered. Scatter the almonds over.

Bake in an oven preheated to 180°C (regular) for about 35 minutes, or until lightly browned on top and you can see the fruit juices bubbling through the crumble topping.

150g plain flour

120g butter, softened and cut into small pieces

5 tablespoons soft brown sugar

2 tablespoons ground almonds

grated zest of 1 lemon

butter for greasing dish

2 cooking apples (granny smith or ballarat)

300g (2 generous cups) well-washed, chopped rhubarb

2 tablespoons unskinned almonds, chopped

SERVES 6

Titbits

Rhubarb started appearing in recipe books in the 19th century. Although it is mainly used in desserts, in some countries it is added to savoury dishes too. I think it makes a great chutney, providing plenty of tang. It has the ability to improve blander fruits: think of an apple crumble made with apples which are bland, maybe floury, or too sweet, but you're stuck with them. Imagine what a cup or so of tangy rhubarb can do to it. (The secret to this crumble is in having plenty of tangy fruit sweetened with enough sugar to make the rhubarb and apple palatable.)
Rhubarb seems to marry well with ginger in any form; it goes well with orange, redcurrant jelly, cinnamon, soft white cheese, yoghurt, custard, ice cream and pastry. And don't forget chutney and savoury uses where a fresh flavour is welcome.

Pick up

Deep pinky-red rhubarb stems rather than very green ones, which tend to be stronger and tougher. The rhubarb should feel firm, not spongy or limp. The ends of the stems should be clean and not in any way slimy. When you get the rhubarb home, lop off the tops of the stems and put the stems in a plastic bag and store them in the refrigerator. They will keep for several days providing the rhubarb was fresh when you purchased it.

Alongside

Cream, custard, ice cream or yoghurt.

Up front

This is great at any temperature, so you can bake it a few hours before serving if you wish to get it done ahead.

X-Factor

Rhubarb stems have some goodies – there's plenty of potassium and calcium – although how much we manage to get of them when we eat rhubarb is debatable. The traces of oxalic acid in the stems seems to inhibit their absorption by the body. The leaves of rhubarb should never be eaten because they contain a lot of oxalic acid and are poisonous. There are plenty of nutrients and fibre from the apples and almonds, making this a worthwhile pudding.

Grilled Gingerbread with Fried Rosemary and Muscat-poached Pears

GINGERBREAD: Sift the dry ingredients into a large bowl, and stir in the preserved ginger. Warm the brown sugar, butter, golden syrup and black treacle in a small pan until dissolved; don't allow the mixture to boil.

Beat the egg and milk together. Combine all the gingerbread ingredients, including the bicarbonate of soda dissolved in milk; mix together until combined but don't beat.

Pour into a non-stick loaf tin (23cm long x 12–13cm wide x 7cm deep) lined with baking paper on the bottom. Bake in an oven preheated to 175°C (regular) for 1¹/₂ hours. If the top starts to colour too quickly, drape a piece of aluminium foil loosely over the surface to deflect the heat. Cool in the tin for 10 minutes, then turn onto a cooling rack.

POACHED PEARS: To prepare the pears, put the sugar in a frying pan or sauté pan with the water and the wine. Heat gently until the sugar is dissolved, then bring to the boil. Boil for 2 minutes, then add the lemon juice. Peel the pears and add them to the pan. Let the syrup boil over them for a minute or two, then lower the heat.

Cook the pears for about 45 minutes, or until tender, turning them over and spooning syrup over them as they cook. When the pears are tender, transfer them to a container and reboil the syrup. Let it reduce for 2–3 minutes, then pour over the pears. Refrigerate when cool.

To present the gingerbread with the poached pears as a dessert, slice and butter each piece of gingerbread lightly, mainly around the edges of the slices. Grill until browning. The gingerbread will feel soft, but it will become crisp as it stands.

To prepare the rosemary, heat a small pan over a medium heat and when it is hot drop in a knob of butter. Put in the rosemary sprigs and fry until browned and crisp.

Serve the gingerbread warm, with poached pears or nectarines on the side, and with fried sprigs of rosemary. Serve with crème fraîche.

Gingerbread
330g plain flour
1 heaped teaspoon ground ginger
¹/₄ teaspoon salt
1 teaspoon baking powder
50g preserved ginger, chopped
170g brown sugar
125g butter
75g golden syrup
120g black treacle
1 egg
300ml milk
1 teaspoon bicarbonate of soda dissolved in a little of the milk

Poached Pears
220g (1 cup) granulated sugar
700ml water
100ml dessert wine (muscat or sauternes)
juice of 1 lemon
6 firm but not woody pears

For Serving
butter
fresh, supple rosemary sprigs
crème fraîche

Titbits
Gingerbread is made using the warming method (the fats and sugars are warmed to combine them, which is different from the creaming method where fat and sugar are whipped together, usually with eggs) and is one of the easier cake-making methods. It's great for cooks who can't stand flour under their fingernails (when making pastry or using the rubbing-in method) or who always curdle creamed cake mixtures!

Essentials
Fresh ground ginger. Ground spices have a short shelf-life. Every few months it is worth going through the pantry and throwing out unused spices because all they're doing is sitting there spoiling and going musty.

Alongside
The full works as recommended here – gingerbread, pears and fried rosemary sprigs with a dollop of crème fraîche or yoghurt. Add a glass of muscat. Have a lie down after.

Up front
The gingerbread is at its sticky best on day three of its life. It's very good on day four. On day five it's still okay, and it's not bad on day six, and it's still edible on day seven. There are not many cakes that keep as well.

X-Factor
Focus on the pears, which have vitamin C, potassium, and fibre.

Butterfly Cakes

125g unsalted butter, cubed then softened
   (it should be really squishy, though not
   oily)
115g ($1/2$ cup) caster sugar
2 medium eggs, at room temperature
120g plain flour
2 teaspoons baking powder
60ml ($1/4$ cup) milk
$1/2$ teaspoon vanilla extract
cream and strawberries for filling, or cream
   and fruit compote or jam
icing sugar for sifting over

MAKES ABOUT 18

PUT the butter in the bowl of a food mixer fitted with the whipping blade and whip it until it is very soft and lighter in colour. Add the sugar and whip until well mixed and pale and creamy coloured; you'll need to stop the machine and scrape the sides of the bowl several times. Break the eggs into a bowl, beat with a fork, and add a little at a time to the whipped butter and sugar with the machine running; scrape the bowl down several times. Continue whipping until the mixture is like a thick whipped cream (if it curdles, just carry on with the recipe). Transfer the mixture to a mixing bowl.

Sift the flour and baking powder together onto a piece of greaseproof paper, then sieve them over the creamed butter and eggs. Fold in with a large spoon, then gently mix in the milk and vanilla extract.

Use two teaspoons to put the mixture in 18 paper cases set inside muffin tins; scoop the mixture up with one of the teaspoons, and use the other to scrape it off into the paper case. Bake for 15 minutes in an oven preheated to 180°C (regular), or until the cakes are an even light golden brown and springy to the touch. Let them cool in the paper cases on a wire rack.

Just before serving, cut a small round off the top of each sponge cake and fill them with cream and jam. Cut the tops in two and poke them into the cream so they stick up like butterfly wings. Alternatively, fill them with cream and a slice of strawberry and one piece of wing – or whatever combination appeals to you.

Titbits

Life without a little whimsy is just dead boring, so get to it and whip up a batch of these childhood favourites – except keep the kids away because they're likely to demolish them when your back is turned.

Pick up

Nothing special – just use fresh ingredients.

Alongside

Serve them as an adult afternoon tea, when no one is expecting such a thing; they'll be a huge hit (bring out the heirloom tea-set, etc, etc).

Up front

Eat them the day you make them, while they're soft and fresh. If need be, weigh up the ingredients the day before making.

X-Factor

None really – sugar and butter whipped into a frenzy with eggs never produced anything much to impress the health police.

Sugar-crusted Cinnamon Sponge with Strawberries and Cream

110g plain flour

pinch of salt

$^1/_2$ teaspoon ground cinnamon

3 medium eggs, at room temperature

125g caster sugar, plus 1 tablespoon for the cream

grated zest of 1 lemon

1 teaspoon dried lavender flowers, crumbled (optional)

150ml cream

small piece of vanilla pod

redcurrant jelly

600g (4 cups) strawberries, hulled

SERVES 8

CHOOSE a cake tin 21cm wide by 5–6cm deep, and line the bottom and sides with baking paper. If the tin is non-stick, line the bottom only.

Sift the flour, salt and cinnamon together onto a piece of greaseproof paper. Break the eggs into a bowl and whisk with a hand-held beater until they are frothy, then whisk in the sugar, a tablespoon at a time. Whisk until the mixture is pale and thick, and continue whisking until it will form ribbons when you stop beating and lift the beaters out of the mixture (the mixture will fall off the beater in a thick trail).

Sift the flour mixture over the top of the whipped egg mixture and carefully fold it in, using a large spoon or rubber scraper, adding the lemon zest and lavender; take care not to knock out the air. Turn the mixture into the prepared tin.

Bake for 15–20 minutes in an oven preheated to 170°C (regular), or until it is springy to the touch and is just starting to pull away from the sides of the tin (it may take as much as 25 minutes, but it is better to keep it soft and moist). Cool for 5 minutes in the tin, then turn the sponge onto a cooling rack and peel off the paper. Let the sponge cool thoroughly before assembling with the cream.

Put the cream in a bowl and flick in the vanilla seeds with the point of a knife. Add 1 tablespoon of sugar and whip until holding its shape. Gently melt the redcurrant jelly (over a very gentle heat or in the microwave); if lumpy, pass the jelly through a sieve. Split the sponge in half with a bread knife and fill with the flavoured cream. Brush the top of the cake with hot redcurrant jelly and arrange the sliced strawberries on top. I like to cut them in quarters and stand them upright on the sponge, tightly packed together. Brush the berries with hot redcurrant jelly.

Titbits

To give the sponge a sugar crust, rub the cake tin lightly with butter. Put a disc of baking paper on the bottom and butter this as well (buttering underneath the paper holds it in place; the bottom of the tin is lined with paper to help turn it out). Put 1 heaped tablespoon of caster sugar in the tin and shake it around the tin to coat the bottom and sides of the tin. Tap out the excess. Repeat this with a tablespoon of flour, tapping out the excess.

Pick up

Dried lavender flowers, but if you can't get them, leave them out; there will be plenty of flavour from the cinnamon, and the lemon will enhance the fruitiness of the strawberries.

Essential

Fresh eggs.

Up front

The sponge is best eaten the day it is made because it contains very little fat (only the egg yolks) and therefore dries out – usually, the more fat a cake contains, the longer it will keep. It is best soon after assembly; if you must make it ahead, keep it refrigerated.

X-Factor

Strawberries and cream on soft sponge cake. Mmmmmm. Have seconds (it's worth it). And strawberries are an excellent source of vitamin C and other antioxidants.

Four-fruit Crumble

SIFT the flour into a bowl and add the butter. Rub in with your fingertips or use a pastry blender until well amalgamated, then mix in 3 tablespoons of the sugar, the almonds and lemon zest. Lightly butter a 20cm round, shallow ovenproof dish.

Halve the feijoas and scoop out the flesh. Put in the dish with the prepared rhubarb. Peel the apple, discard the core and slice finely. Add to the dish with the sliced banana and mix in the rest of the brown sugar.

Spoon the crumble topping over the fruit, ensuring all the fruit is covered.

Bake in an oven preheated to 180°C (regular) for about 35 minutes, or until lightly browned on top and you can see the fruit juices bubbling through the crumble topping.

150g plain flour

120g butter, softened and cut into small pieces

5 tablespoons soft brown sugar

2 tablespoons ground almonds

grated zest of 1 lemon

butter for greasing

6 large feijoas

150g chopped rhubarb (about 1 generous cup), well washed

1 cooking apple (granny smith or ballarat)

1 banana

SERVES 6

Titbits

The feijoa is a green thin-skinned fruit, round to oval in shape, with a powerful heady fragrance that is a mix of pineapple and pear, with a little banana and melon, and, some say, a whiff of strawberry too. The cream coloured flesh, apart from the jellied seeds, is granular, like a pear. The green skin is not normally eaten, but it can be grated and used like lemon rind.

Feijoas are best eaten soon after picking, while they have their highest concentration of vitamin C and before they start developing any internal browning or off-flavours. The fruit is at its peak when the inside jellied sections are clear. They're delicious on their own, but there's plenty else you can do with them. Feijoas can be frozen; peel them, put in a freezer bag and freeze for up to 6 months.

Pick up

Feijoas, which probably means you need to be in the southern hemisphere to make this crumble; although there is a big export trade from New Zealand. If you can't get them, make Apple and Rhubarb Crumble (see page 143) instead.

Alongside

Cream, custard, ice cream or yoghurt.

Up front

The crumble can be made and cooked an hour or two before serving.

X-Factor

The exotic perfume this crumble gives off as it cooks (the mix of feijoa and banana does it) is sure to raise the excitement level at the table. But if all the crumble doesn't get consumed in one sitting – there's a treat in store for breakfast. Serving left-over crumble for breakfast might be considered decadent, but it's worth every calorie. And there's plenty of goodness in the ground almonds and fruit content, so you don't need to do penance after this pudding.

Rice and Apricot Puddings with Brûlée Topping

100g (¹/₂ cup, tightly packed) dried apricots
175g (³/₄ cup) medium grain rice
600ml milk
1 piece vanilla pod
175g (³/₄ cup) caster sugar
juice of 1 lemon
200ml cream

SERVES 6

PUT the apricots in a bowl and cover with boiling water. Leave them to soften for 2–3 hours. Drain, reserving the soaking liquid, then chop them coarsely.

Put the unwashed rice, milk, vanilla pod (scrape the seeds into the rice and milk first), and 4 tablespoons of the sugar in a shallow ovenproof dish. Cook for 1 hour in an oven preheated to 150°C (regular). The rice should have absorbed nearly all the milk and be creamy but not gluggy. Stir in the lemon juice, cream and chopped apricots and add enough of the reserved apricot liquid to make the rice moist and sloppy (I usually need all the apricot juice – the mixture does stiffen on chilling). Spoon the rice into six ramekins and smooth the top. When cool, chill thoroughly.

Spread a thick layer of sugar on top of each pudding. Cook under a very hot grill, or brown with a small gas blowtorch until the sugar melts and turns pale gold in colour. Chill again until serving time.

Titbits

These are the Rolls Royce of rice puds – and they're dead easy to make.

Pick up

Australian calrose rice, but if you can't get this, any medium grain rice will do. Investing in a small gas blowtorch makes browning the top easy.

Essential

Quality dried apricots that have got a decent tang – they balance the richness of the puddings and merge beautifully with the caramel topping.

Alongside

Grab a bottle of luscious late-harvest riesling or sauternes to go with it.

Up front

The puds can be made up to a day ahead. As they wait in the fridge to be eaten the caramel topping softens and starts to seep its way through the pudding. Cor! They're outrageously good!

X-Factor

Dried apricots contain the antioxidant beta-carotene, as well as iron, potassium and manganese. Lemon provides vitamin C. This good news balances the naughty ingredients (sugar and cream) so you can feel reasonably good about scoffing one of these!

sweetie pies

Chocolate Nut Cake

60g unsalted butter

375g dark chocolate, broken into squares

2/3 cup pecans, walnuts or skinned almonds

45g (1/3 cup) plain flour

75g (1/3 cup) caster sugar

2 tablespoons Cointreau

60ml (1/4 cup) water

6 medium eggs, at room temperature

pinch of cream of tartar

SERVES AT LEAST 8

FIRST prepare the cake tin. Line the sides and base of a 23cm round cake tin with non-stick baking paper.

Put the butter and chocolate in a small saucepan and melt carefully over a low heat, stirring until smooth.

Put the nuts, flour and caster sugar together in the bowl of a food processor, or in a liquidiser, and process briefly until the nuts are coarsely ground. Turn into a bowl and mix in two-thirds of the melted butter and chocolate mixture, the Cointreau and water.

Separate the eggs, putting the whites in a grease-free bowl and the yolks in a small bowl. Beat the yolks for a minute or two, then blend into the chocolate mixture. Whip the egg whites and cream of tartar together until firm, but not stiff and dry. Mix a large spoonful of the whipped whites into the chocolate mixture, then carefully fold in the rest with a large spoon. Spoon into the prepared tin.

Bake in an oven preheated to 180°C (regular), for 25–30 minutes, or until firmish to the touch. Cool in the tin, turn out onto a cake rack and peel off the paper. Leave until nearly cool.

Gently rewarm the remaining chocolate and butter mixture, then spread over the top and sides of the cake, using a flat-bladed knife. Leave at room temperature until set. (Don't refrigerate the cake as the chocolate topping loses its gloss when chilled.)

Titbits

Grinding the nuts with the flour and sugar stops them turning oily; oily nuts make the texture of the cake dense and heavy.

Pick up

Fresh nuts. Rancid, bitter walnuts will ruin the cake (maybe even you – they're toxic!). Walnut skins, even on fresh nuts, are faintly bitter, so flick off as much skin as you can. Almonds are the best in my opinion, because they don't go rancid as quickly as walnuts and pecans.

Essential

Fabulous chocolate. This is not a place to use cheap chocolate 'buttons'. I use Valrhona for its rich taste, spreadability and gloss.

Alongside

Huge dollops of cream. If you're going to pay for a passion, you may as well be 100% guilty!

Up front

The cake keeps well for a day or two, but resist the temptation to put it in the refrigerator because the chocolate coating will lose its lovely gloss. If this happens, and a very cool kitchen can be the culprit, give it a quick buzz over with a hairdryer and see if you can return it to its former glory (well, it works for me sometimes!).

X-Factor

Butter, sugar and liqueur can't generally be considered healthy – thank God for the nuts and chocolate! Quality dark chocolate is rich in antioxidants, and yes, chocolate is an aphrodisiac, so mete out the biggest slice to the one you fancy the most.

Coconut Ice Cream with Fruit in Lemongrass Syrup

Coconut Ice Cream

4 medium eggs, at room temperature

100g caster sugar

200ml thick coconut cream (see below)

300ml cream, lightly whipped

grated zest of 1 lemon

Fruit in Lemongrass Syrup

100g granulated sugar

225ml water

1 stalk lemongrass, bruised with a mallet

1 thick slice fresh ginger

a selection of fresh seasonal fruit such as
    papaya, mango, banana, plums, peaches,
    nectarines, strawberries, pineapple

1 can lychees in syrup, drained

SERVES 8

TO make the ice cream, separate the eggs, putting the whites in a grease-free bowl and the yolks in a large bowl. Beat the yolks with 70g of the caster sugar until thick and creamy and pale yellow in colour. Stir in the coconut cream, then the whipped cream, and mix gently until well blended. Whisk the egg whites until very stiff, then add the rest of the sugar and beat for 30 seconds. Mix into the egg yolk mixture with the lemon zest, using a large spoon; do not beat.

Transfer the mixture to a mould and freeze for at least 6 hours (it's at its peak when nearly frozen).

If making the ice cream ahead of time, allow it to soften in the refrigerator for 1 hour before serving. Scoop it onto serving plates and serve with the fruit salad, or put scoops of it piled high in tall chilled glasses. Alternatively, make it in individual ramekins. To serve with meringues, sandwich two meringues with scoops of ice cream.

To make the syrup, put the sugar in a small pan with the water. Dissolve the sugar in the water over a low heat, stirring gently with a metal spoon so the sugar doesn't settle on the bottom of the pan. As soon as the sugar is dissolved, add the lemongrass and ginger slice and bring to the boil. Boil for 5 minutes then cool. Strain and use when cool.

Prepare the fruit by peeling, slicing, removing seeds, chopping, etc, then put in a bowl with the syrup and leave to macerate for 1 hour before serving.

Titbits

I credit my South Australian friend Margaret Johnson for this ice cream recipe. An ice cream churn will definitely improve the texture of it, but it's not essential. The trick is to move the ice cream from the freezer to the refrigerator about 40 minutes before serving, which allows it to soften without melting. I use a hand-held electric beater to mix the whites for the ice cream.

When making the sugar syrup, don't let the water boil until the sugar is dissolved, or the sugar may crystallise on standing. The syrup can be stored for several weeks in the refrigerator.

Pick up

Fresh lemongrass – buy a small root piece and smash it with a mallet to release its fragrance and flavour. If not available, use a couple of sliced fresh lemon leaves. Canned fruit in a fresh fruit salad? You betcha if it's lychees! The flavour of the lychees with the coconut ice cream is quite exotic.

Essential

Coconut cream – it's richer than coconut milk.

It gives a wonderfully strong coconutty taste. Let the can stand for an hour before using so that the cream can float to the top of the liquid. Use any remaining coconut liquid in a rice or chicken dish.

Alongside

Nothing else is needed – you've got crunch, creaminess, juiciness, fragrance and flavour – but meringues would be a delicious extra (see page 157)!

Up front

Both the ice cream and syrup can be made ahead. Most of the fruit can be prepared several hours ahead (not strawberries, which soften too quickly), put in a bowl with the syrup and lychees, and kept covered and refrigerated until serving. Add any berries at serving time.

X-Factor

White sugar, cream, coconut cream – hmmm. At least the fruit is good for you!

Almond Meringue and Berry Flan

MAKE the pastry first. Sift the flour into a large bowl and add the butter and shortening. Cut into the flour with two knives or a pastry blender, then use your fingertips to rub in the fat until the mixture resembles coarse breadcrumbs.

Stir the ground almonds and sugar through. Mix the egg yolk, water and vanilla extract together, then pour into the dry ingredients. Blend in with a knife and work the mixture together with your hands. Knead lightly. Roll on a floured surface and line into a 21cm-diameter flan ring. Chill well. If the pastry feels sticky after making, wrap in plastic food wrap and chill for 20 minutes before rolling out.

Next make the meringue. Beat the egg whites with an electric beater until foamy, then dribble in the caster sugar. Beat until the mixture forms stiff peaks. Meanwhile, remove the pastry case from the refrigerator and prick the base with a fork, then scatter the raspberries over it.

Fold the almonds into the whipped egg whites. Spread over the raspberries, keeping the mixture in from the pastry edge as it swells a little during baking.

Bake in an oven preheated to 180°C (fanbake) for 30 minutes. If the meringue colours too quickly, drape a piece of aluminium foil over the top to deflect the top heat. Remove the flan from the oven, leave for 5 minutes, then slide onto a cooling rack.

Put the flaked almonds in a shallow dish and toast in the oven for 4-5 minutes.

Spread about two-thirds over the meringue, then spoon the cream on top of the flan in dollops. Scatter the almonds over and serve.

Pastry
170g plain flour
90g butter, pliable, cut into small chunks
30g shortening
45g (about 6 tablespoons) ground almonds
45g (about 4 tablespoons) caster sugar
1 large egg yolk
2 tablespoons ice-cold water
2–3 drops vanilla extract

Meringue
2 small egg whites
120g caster sugar
120g ground almonds, toasted

1 cup (about 150g) raspberries

To Decorate
300ml cream
1 teaspoon caster sugar
2–3 drops vanilla extract
2 tablespoons flaked almonds

SERVES 6 OR MORE

Titbits

This is a serious dessert with several stages, but it can be made in advance. Toast the almonds while the flan is cooking. Put the almonds in an ovenproof dish and cook for about 5 minutes until lightly coloured. Cool and store airtight.

If your oven doesn't brown pastry well, or does not have a good bottom heat, it may be worth baking the pastry blind for 15 minutes. Finishing the dessert with rosettes of cream has to be considered pretty retro these days (it was de rigeur in the seventies). Personally, I couldn't do it, and prefer to plop the cream from a spoon.

Up front

The flan can be prepared several hours ahead; when cool, store in the pantry, not the fridge. Before serving, whip the cream very lightly, adding sugar and vanilla extract as it thickens.

X-Factor

This seriously good dessert will win you points at your next dinner party.
If you can't stand the idea of using shortening in the pastry (it makes it very light), use all butter. Raspberries are a particularly good fruit, with lots of vitamin C and other antioxidants, some folate and manganese, and loads of dietary fibre.

Sticky Lemon Slice

225g unsalted butter, softened

70g icing sugar

275g plain flour

400g granulated sugar

4 medium eggs, beaten together

4 tablespoons plain flour

1 teaspoon baking powder

grated zest of 2 lemons

90ml lemon juice, strained

icing sugar for dusting

MAKES ABOUT 28 SQUARES

PUT the softened butter in the bowl of a food processor and process until whipped, then add the icing sugar and process until light in colour (creamed). Sprinkle the flour over and process until the mixture starts to form a ball. Tip into a non-stick Swiss roll tin (32cm x 21cm), with the bottom lined with baking paper, and press flat. If the mixture is sticky, keep your fingers dusted with plain flour.

Bake in an oven preheated to 170°C (regular) for 15 minutes, then remove from the oven. While the base is cooling, make the topping.

Tip the granulated sugar into the bowl of a food processor and pour in the eggs. Process for 1 minute. Transfer the mixture to a bowl, then sprinkle the flour and baking powder over, and add the lemon zest and juice. Mix together with a large spoon.

Pour the mixture on top of the base (it will fill the tin), then return it to the oven and bake for a further 30–35 minutes, or until golden in colour and firmish to the touch. Cool in the tin, then dust with icing sugar and cut into squares. Transfer to an airtight container when cool.

Titbits

This super-delectable, sweet-but-tart 'slice' is quickly made in a food processor. If you don't have a food processor, cream the butter and icing sugar and work in the flour. For the topping, whip the sugar and eggs together with a rotary beater.

Alongside

A pot of tea so you can take long draughts to wash away the sweetness. Having said that, lemon does amazing things with coffee, so a slice with a cup of espresso coffee is gorgeous too.

X-Factor

Think of all that lemon juice and how good it is for you and forget about the butter and sugar. Go on, have another slice!

Weeping Raspberry Fairy Cake

melted butter for greasing the tin
75g plain flour
pinch of salt
2 teaspoons cream of tartar
6 medium egg whites
175g (³/₄ cup) caster sugar
1 teaspoon vanilla extract
1 tablespoon lemon juice
300ml cream
icing sugar for dusting
2 cups (about 300g) fresh raspberries
50g (about ¹/₂ cup) icing sugar

SERVES 8

THIS is best made in a 20cm round cake tin, about 6–7cm deep, and preferably with a removable base. Brush the sides and bottom lightly with melted butter.

Sift the flour, salt and 1 teaspoon of the cream of tartar onto a piece of paper. Whisk the egg whites until stiff, then sift in the other teaspoon of cream of tartar and 1 tablespoon of the caster sugar. Whisk in the remaining sugar a little at a time. Sprinkle the vanilla extract and lemon juice on and mix in. Sift half the flour mixture over the surface of the egg whites and fold in carefully with a large spoon. Repeat with the rest of the flour mixture.

Spoon the mixture into the tin, level the surface with a knife, then bake in an oven preheated to 190°C (regular) for 15–20 minutes. If it starts browning too quickly, lower the heat. Lower the heat to 170°C and bake for a further 15–20 minutes, or until the cake is a light golden brown, springy to the touch and pulling away from the sides of the tin. Remove from the oven and cool in the tin for 10 minutes. Carefully invert onto a cooling rack.

When the cake is cool, cut into three rounds with a serrated knife. Put the bottom of the sponge on a serving plate. Lightly whip the cream until it is just holding shape, but still falling off the whisk in dollops. Spread one-third of the cream over the sponge base. Spoon half the raspberries (see below) on top of the cream, then top with the second round of sponge. Cover with another portion of cream and the rest of the raspberries, then put the top sponge layer in place.

Sift icing sugar over the top. Put the rest of the cream in a piping bag fitted with a 'rose' nozzle and pipe rosettes of cream around the edge of the sponge, or serve it separately. Serve immediately, or refrigerate until required.

RASPBERRY PREPARATION: Put the raspberries in a bowl and sprinkle most of the icing sugar over them. Leave for about an hour, stirring once or twice, or until the juices run. Tip the raspberries into a sieve and use. Reserve the juice to serve with the cake.

Titbits

Although this cake is filled with lashings of whipped cream, it is not rich, thanks to the fresh taste of the raspberries. It is wonderfully light and a real summer treat. It will keep in the refrigerator for 2–3 days after making.

Pick up

Fresh raspberries in summer – it's best made with these. But for a winter version frozen berries are also very good. If you want to serve a dessert wine with this, choose a botrytised riesling, or a fruity bubbly, something like an asti spumante.

Up front

I actually prefer this cake several hours after it has been assembled because the raspberries weep into the cake rounds and through the cream. The best way to store a cream-filled cake (cream absorbs odours from other food in the refrigerator) is in a large plastic container with a lid.

X-Factor

Three cheers for raspberries – they're full of fibre, and have a good whack of vitamin C and other antioxidants, some folate and manganese!

Pecan and Apricot Tart

Pastry

75g butter, softened

115g (½ cup) caster sugar

1 egg yolk

30g (¼ cup) shelled pecans, finely chopped

120g (1 cup) plain flour

pinch of salt

Filling

90g butter, softened

75g (½ cup) soft brown sugar

100g (¼ cup) honey, warmed until liquid

3 eggs

½ cup shelled pecans, coarsely chopped

60g (¼ cup) dried apricots, roughly chopped, then soaked for 15 minutes in boiling water

SERVES 6-8

MAKE the pastry first. Beat the butter until smooth (easiest done with a hand-held electric beater), then add the sugar. Beat until creamed and white, then beat in the egg yolk. Mix in the nuts, sift the flour and salt over and blend by hand into a ball. Knead in the bowl until smooth, then wrap in plastic food wrap and chill until firm.

Press the pastry into a 23cm flan dish, prick the surface all over and chill again until firm.

Crumple a piece of clean tissue paper and line into the flan ring, filling with baking beans or rice. Bake for 10 minutes at 180°C (fanbake), remove the beans and paper, and bake for another 5 minutes. While the pastry is baking, make the filling.

Beat the butter until smooth, as described above, then add the sugar. Beat until creamed, then add the honey, then the eggs, one by one, beating well after each addition. Don't worry if the mixture separates; carry on with the recipe. Mix the pecans and drained apricots through, then pour into the pastry case.

Bake for about 20 minutes at 180°C (fanbake), or until the filling is set and golden (be careful not to let it burn). Cool before serving.

Titbits

Delicious, delicious, delicious! Nutty, creamy pecans and tart lemony apricots with honey and brown sugar make a very moreish tart.

Essential

Fresh pecans.

Alongside

Cream, liquid or whipped, or yoghurt. If you're looking for a special dessert wine, splash out on a sauterne or Beaumes-de-Venise. Another option is a glass of raisiny Vin Santo.

Up front

The pastry can be made ahead and frozen before baking; thaw briefly, then bake.

X-Factor

This scores high on the 'yum' scales. I think it's the way the apricots bite their way through the honeyed nutty filling that does it. Dried apricots have plenty of antioxidants (especially beta-carotene) and minerals.

Apple Jalousie

ROLL the pastry into a rectangle 0.5cm thick, on a lightly floured board. Cut the pastry into two pieces, making one about 3cm longer than the other. Now roll the smaller piece the same size as the larger one. Trim the edges to neaten, then place the thinner piece of pastry on a covered baking sheet (use a non-stick baking sheet or baking paper). Place in the refrigerator to chill. Chill the other piece of pastry on a tray.

Peel the apples and quickly slice into very thin pieces. Dampen a border on the pastry being used for the base (the thinner piece) and arrange the sliced apple on top, leaving the border clear. Scatter the sultanas over.

Now take the other piece of pastry and fold it in two lengthways. Using a very sharp knife dipped in flour, cut ribbons across the pastry through the folded centre, but not quite to the cut edges. Open out the pastry carefully and place it on top of the apples. Press the edges together firmly. Use a small sharp knife to lightly cut the edges of the pastry. This opens up the layers of the pastry without breaking the seal, and allows the pastry to rise and flake.

Brush the pastry with the lightly beaten egg white, sprinkle the caster sugar over, then scatter the nuts over the top. Bake at 200°C (fanbake) for about 20 minutes, then lower the oven temperature to 180°C. If the pastry and nuts have coloured sufficiently on top, cover loosely with a piece of aluminium foil. Bake for a further 10–15 minutes. Slide onto a cooling rack.

Make the glaze. Put the jam and lemon juice into a small saucepan and bring to the boil, stirring, then pass the glaze through a metal sieve. Discard any lumps and check the consistency. It should fall off the spoon easily and not be so thick that it is difficult to spread. If it is too thin, reduce it over a high heat; if it is too thick, thin it with water.

Work with the glaze while it is very hot. Brush the top of the jalousie liberally with the hot apricot glaze, returning the pan to the element from time to time to keep it just under boiling point. Serve the jalousie cool.

400g purchased flaky or rough-puff pastry, thawed if frozen
4 large apples (granny smith or ballarat)
35g (¼ cup) sultanas
1 egg white, lightly beaten
caster sugar
25g (¼ cup) flaked almonds

Apricot Glaze
375g small jar apricot jam
1 teaspoon lemon juice

SERVES 6-8 GENEROUSLY

Titbits
Finishing a winter's meal with an apple and pastry dessert might seem predictable, but reserve your judgement until you've tried this one. The pastry preparation may sound difficult, but all you've done is cut a piece of pastry through the folded side not quite all the way to the cut edges. When the piece of pastry is opened up, it's like a slatted shutter with an uncut frame around all sides. As the pastry cooks, the 'slats' (strips of pastry) puff and separate, revealing some of the filling, and become crisp as the steam from the apples can escape freely.
Choose an inexpensive apricot jam for the glaze. The lemon juice helps to cut the sweetness. Leftover glaze stores in the refrigerator indefinitely.

Pick up
If you like making pastry, you could make your own flaky or rough puff – but very few will know the difference between homemade and commercially made. Buy the best pastry available is my advice.

Alongside
Custard or ice cream is the best, but cream or crème fraîche both work, and a glass of late-harvest riesling makes it even more delicious.

Up front
Make the pastry, wrap it in plastic food wrap and chill it, then cut the shapes and chill it again. If using ready-made pastry, cut it and chill.

X-Factor
There's a certain comfort factor about homemade pastry desserts. This is the sort of thing I'd put together quite quickly for the family in winter using ready-made pastry, although it would not be out of place at a special dinner.

Dolores' German Apple Cake

PUT the softened butter in the bowl of an electric cake mixer and mix until soft and loose. Add the sugar, eggs and vanilla extract and beat until thick and creamy; don't worry too much if it separates – it all comes together in the end!

Sift the flour and baking powder together onto a piece of greaseproof paper, then mix in, a quarter at a time, adding the milk.

Transfer the mixture to a 23cm round cake tin, the bottom and sides lined with baking paper. Smooth the top of the batter. Partially slice the pieces of apple, about three-quarters of the way through each piece, open them up like fans and press them deeply into the cake batter; make two layers of apples.

Mix the tablespoon of caster sugar and the cinnamon together and sprinkle the top with cinnamon sugar.

Bake in an oven preheated to 180°C (regular) for 50 minutes, until golden brown. If the apples are still a little hard, cover the cake loosely with aluminium foil and continue cooking for 10 minutes more.

Cool in the tin for 15 minutes, then turn out onto a plate. Serve warmish dusted with icing sugar.

125g unsalted butter, cubed, then softened
125g caster sugar
3 medium eggs, at room temperature, lightly beaten together
1 teaspoon vanilla extract
200g plain flour
2 teaspoons baking powder
2 tablespoons milk
1kg (6–7 apples) cooking apples (granny smith, ballarat, etc) peeled, cored and quartered
1 tablespoon caster sugar
$1/4$ teaspoon ground cinnamon
icing sugar

SERVES 8 OR MORE

Titbits

This is fabulously moist with loads of apple. It can be made just as well with a hand-held electric beater, and although I haven't tried it, I'm sure it would come up trumps if made in a food processor with the whipping blade. Who is Dolores? She's my German sister-in-law and she's nearly as delicious as this cake!

Essential

Good apples – they need to retain their shape after cooking (not turn to fluff) and have a sharp bite to them, which gives the cake some interest. However, you don't want dry fibrous apples that take an age to soften.

Alongside

A pool of cream, a dollop of yoghurt, a blob of crème fraîche – all will work.

Up front

As with most cakes, the tin preparation and weighing of ingredients can be done the day before baking the cake (handy to remember if you're trying to save yourself time on baking day). The butter and eggs should be at room temperature because the butter will be easier to whip, and the two fats (butter and egg yolks) will be more inclined to cosy-up together in the bowl. Peel the apples at the last minute because they discolour if left after peeling.

X-Factor

A cake's a cake – at least this one has got plenty of apples, which are a very good antioxidant!

Vacherin

3 medium egg whites
165g caster sugar
about 300ml cream
piece of vanilla pod
icing sugar for dusting

MAKES TEN 10CM PIPED MERINGUE
ROUNDS

WHISK the egg whites in a totally grease-free copper, china, glass or stainless steel bowl until they are stiff and can stand in peaks on an upturned whisk. Add 2 tablespoons of the measured sugar and whisk in for 30 seconds. Sprinkle the rest of the sugar over and fold it in carefully with a large metal spoon until just mixed through.

Put some of the mixture in a piping bag fitted with a plain 'eclair' piping nozzle (the old $1/2$" size). Pipe out ten 10cm-diameter circles on trays lined with baking paper, starting in the centre and piping in a spiral. If it helps, trace circles on the baking paper using a pencil, (then turn the baking paper over so the pencil marking doesn't come in contact with the meringue).

Bake in an oven preheated to 120°C (regular), for at least an hour; swap the position of the trays once during cooking. If the meringues brown in the first 15 minutes, the temperature is too high, but if they are sticky to the touch after 30 minutes, the temperature is too low.

Cook until a very pale coffee colour and crisp to the touch. The meringues should be easy to remove from the paper; if they are tacky, they need longer cooking. Carefully peel the paper off the vacherin rounds and put them back on the paper, bottoms up. Return them to the oven, turn off the heat and leave to dry in the cooling oven (remember to remove them before switching on the oven).

About 1 hour before serving, whip the cream lightly, flicking in some seeds from a piece of vanilla pod and adding a teaspoon of sugar. Sandwich the vacherin rounds together with cream and arrange on a serving plate. Leave for 1 hour so that the cream can soften the meringues a little. Before serving, dust the tops with icing sugar. Alternatively, sandwich the rounds of meringue with scoops of Coconut Ice Cream (see page 156).

Titbits

I'm not big on sweet things, except for a couple of weaknesses – meringues with cream being one of them! However, I hate those egg-whitey goobeyish imitation pavlovas. Try this classic vacherin recipe in place of pavlova and wait for the compliments. Make up the meringue as described, then pipe out two 20cm rounds and cook for at least 1 hour at 120°C (regular). Sandwich the meringue rounds with cream a couple of hours before serving to allow the meringue to soften a little (otherwise it shatters when you try to cut it). Just before serving, pile the fruit in lemon-grass syrup (see page 156), without too much juice, on top of the vacherin; it looks gorgeous. Serve the juice separately.
The best meringue Suisse (that's the name for this type of meringue) is made using a copper bowl and a large balloon whisk with plenty of elbow grease. This way you incorporate a lot of air (a cake-mixer makes light work of the job but it produces a denser, less aerated meringue that can be chewy, not crisp).

Up front

Meringues can be made a day or two in advance and will keep for months in the freezer. If freezing the meringues, put them in rigid containers to prevent them shattering. If making a whole vacherin, you can fill it with cream ahead of time, but don't add fruit until serving time. Don't fill the small vacherin with ice cream until ready to serve.

X-Factor

Don't be silly – there's enough white sugar in here to send you spinning into orbit!
It's empty food, and there's no reason to eat such a confection – except for the way it teases and pleases the palate with its crunchy sugary flakes and voluptuous smooth cream. And once you start, you can't stop until it's all gobbled up.

Almond and Yoghurt Cake

350g (2¹/₂ cups) plain flour
2 teaspoons baking powder
¹/₂ teaspoon bicarbonate of soda
150g butter, softened
125g caster sugar
3 eggs, beaten with a fork
250ml (1 cup) plain unsweetened yoghurt
140g (1 cup) coarsely ground almonds
grated zest of 1 lemon

Syrup

440g (2 cups) granulated sugar
250ml (1 cup) water
strained juice of 1 lemon

SERVES AT LEAST 10

BUTTER a shallow ovenproof dish (Pyrex or similar) 33cm long x 23cm wide x 5cm deep. Sift the flour, baking powder and bicarbonate of soda onto a large sheet of greaseproof paper.

Cream the butter well, beat in the sugar a little at a time and beat until light and fluffy. Add the beaten eggs a little at a time, beating well after each addition. About halfway through beating, add a tablespoon of the dry ingredients to help stabilise the mixture.

Mix in one-third of the dry ingredients, then one-third of the yoghurt, and continue adding and mixing in the same way until all the ingredients are mixed in. Don't beat.

Fold in the almonds and lemon zest, then turn the mixture into the prepared dish. Smooth the top, then bake in an oven preheated to 170°C (regular) for about 45 minutes, or until firm to the touch and lightly golden.

To make the syrup, put the sugar, water and lemon juice in a saucepan and stir over a gentle heat until the sugar is dissolved. Boil, uncovered, for 5 minutes.

Make a dozen small holes in the cake with a fine skewer, then pour the syrup over the cake. Leave the cake to cool and absorb the syrup (about 6 hours). Cut into small diamonds or squares and top with whipped cream.

Titbits

Yoghurt gives this sweet, nutty Middle Eastern almond cake a wonderfully light texture. I've cut the sugar content down considerably, especially in the syrup – my first attempt was so sugary that my tooth cavities still twinge at the memory. Remember that you must let the cake sit for 6 hours before serving.

Alongside

This is a good dessert to serve after a meal with Middle Eastern flavours. Serve with yoghurt.

Up front

Perfect for entertaining; it's got to be made hours in advance.

X-Factor

The cake contains a cup each of yoghurt and ground almonds, and lemon juice too. Insist on serving it with more yoghurt and turn this into a moderately healthy cake.

Lemon Sponge Cake

PUT the butter in the warmed bowl of a food processor bowl and whip until 'loose'. Add the caster sugar little by little and process for 5 minutes until lighter in colour and aerated.

Have the eggs ready, broken into a small bowl and lightly beaten with a fork. Dribble the eggs into the whipped butter and sugar a little at a time, with the machine set on full speed. After about half the eggs have been beaten in, add 2 tablespoons of the measured flour to help stabilise the mixture. Lastly, blend in the lemon zest.

Turn the mixture into a large bowl and sift in half the flour, but all the baking powder. Fold in with a large spoon, then sift in the rest of the flour mix and gently stir it in.

Turn the mixture into a shallow gratin or roasting dish, lined on the base with buttered baking paper (the dish should be about 30cm long by 23cm wide and 4cm deep). Smooth the top of the mixture with a spatula. Bake at 170°C (regular) for about 30–40 minutes. When cooked the cake should be an even golden brown, feel springy to the touch and come away from the sides of the dish.

While the cake is still warm, poke dozens of small holes in the surface with a fine skewer and dribble the lemon juice over. Leave for 10 minutes, then turn it onto a cooling rack and peel off the paper.

Sift the icing sugar into a bowl and mix in enough lemon juice to form a 'pourable' icing. Spread on top of the cake using a flat-bladed knife. Cut into squares for serving once the icing has set.

250g soft butter, cut into cubes
250g caster sugar
5 eggs, at room temperature
250g plain flour
grated zest of 2 lemons
2 level teaspoons baking powder
juice of 3 lemons, strained

Icing
200g icing sugar, sifted
extra lemon juice, strained

SERVES 10 OR MORE

Titbits

This makes a large, light lemony cake. It is easily made in a large food processor. If you don't have a food processor, cream the butter and sugar with a hand-held electric beater, whip in the eggs a little at a time, then fold in the dry ingredients and lemon zest.

Alongside

You could have this on its own with tea or coffee, or you could serve it with a fresh fruit salad for dessert.

Up front

The cake can be made several hours before serving. It keeps well for 2–3 days.

X-Factor

You can feel good about eating this because it is light and lemony. Everyone is allowed cake occasionally.

weights and measurements

Grams to Ounces and vice versa

General			Exact		
30g	=	1oz	1oz	=	28.35g
60g	=	2oz	2oz	=	56.70g
90g	=	3oz	3oz	=	85.05g
120g	=	4oz	4oz	=	113.04g
150g	=	5oz	5oz	=	141.08g
180g	=	6oz	6oz	=	170.01g
210g	=	7oz	7oz	=	198.04g
230g	=	8oz	8oz	=	226.08g
260g	=	9oz	9oz	=	255.01g
290g	=	10oz	10oz	=	283.05g
320g	=	11oz	11oz	=	311.08g
350g	=	12oz	12oz	=	340.02g
380g	=	13oz	13oz	=	368.05g
410g	=	14oz	14oz	=	396.09g
440g	=	15oz	15oz	=	425.02g
470g	=	16oz	16oz	=	453.06g

Recipes based on these (International Units)
rounded values

Liquid Measurements

25ml (28.4ml)	=	1fl oz					
150ml (142ml)	=	5fl oz	=	$^1/_4$ pint	=	1 gill
275ml (284ml)	=	10fl oz	=	$^1/_2$ pint		
425ml (426ml)	=	15fl oz	=	$^3/_4$ pint		
575ml (568ml)	=	20fl oz	=	1 pint		

Spoon Measures

$^1/_4$ teaspoon	=	1.25ml
$^1/_2$ teaspoon	=	2.5ml
1 teaspoon	=	5ml
1 tablespoon	=	15ml

In NZ, SA, USA and UK 1 tablespoon = 15ml
In Australia 1 tablespoon = 20ml
1 tablespoon butter equals about 10g

Measurements
cm to approx inches

0.5cm	=	$^1/_4$"	5cm	=	2"
1.25cm	=	$^1/_2$"	7.5cm	=	3"
2.5cm	=	1"	10cm	=	4"

Cake Tin Sizes
cm to approx inches

15cm	=	6"	23cm	=	9"
18cm	=	7"	25cm	=	10"
20cm	=	8"			

Oven Temperatures

Celsius	Fahrenheit	Gas	
110°C	225°F	$^1/_4$	very cool
120°C	250°F	$^1/_2$	
140°C	275°F	1	cool
150°C	300°F	2	
170°C	325°F	3	moderate
180°C	350°F	4	
190°C	375°F	5	moderately hot
200°C	400°F	6	
220°C	425°F	7	hot
230°C	450°F	8	
240°C	475°F	9	very hot

Abbreviations

g	gram
kg	kilogram
mm	millimetre
cm	centimetre
ml	millilitre
°C	degrees Celsius
°F	degrees Fahrenheit

American-Imperial

in	inch
lb	pound
oz	ounce

recipe index

Acknowledgements

ALTHOUGH the author gets most of the credit for a book, there are always many people behind the scenes beavering away. I have a truly fabulous team, starting with New Holland Publishers: Renée Lang, Belinda Cooke and Andrew Rumbles – they've been super-charged up over this project and it is reflected in the end result. Barbara Nielsen has done her usual excellent job of editing the manuscript, and thanks must also go to the typesetter, Kate Greenaway, for fast-tracking the layout. Christine Hansen's stunning design has provided the perfect backdrop for Ian Batchelor's gorgeous photographs. Ian always does a cracker of a job, but he's really excelled himself this time and I want to lick the pages!

Ray Richards, my literary agent, has aided this project with his expert advice, great humour and friendship. And my immediate family, Remo, Luca and Ilaria, and my ever-increasing extended family and special friends, have helped by being guinea-pigs, sometimes willing and sometimes unwilling, in perfecting the recipes. It's been great fun doing this book, the best ever. Thanks everyone!

Of course, to make sure I got my facts right, we called in an expert. Dr Carolyn Lister, a scientist working with Crop & Food Research in New Zealand, gave the health claims a good going over. Carolyn is leading a research programme investigating the health benefits of plant-based foods. Antioxidants are her baby.

Two companies, with whom I have had a long and pleasant relationship, loaned props for the photographs:
Milly's Kitchen Shop of Ponsonby, Auckland, New Zealand Tel. +64 9 376-1550
The Studio of Tableware, Auckland, New Zealand Tel. +64 9 638-8082

Special thanks to Lufthansa German Airlines, New Zealand, for their assistance in travel to Europe.